The Cleveland Way

Yorkshire Moors and Coast Footpath

Described by
Bill Cowley

Dalesman Books
1987

The Dalesman Publishing Company Ltd.,
Clapham, via Lancaster, LA2 8EB.

First published 1969
Sixth edition 1987

ISBN: 0 85206 906 5

To Mary, who walked this way with me so
long ago; and to Jean, who walks it with
me now.

Printed in Great Britain by Fretwell & Cox Limited,
Goulbourne Street, Keighley, West Yorkshire BD21 1PZ.

Contents

Maps and sketches by Jean Cowley.

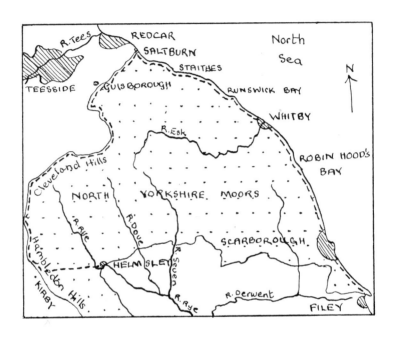

Introduction

Creation of a Long-Distance Footpath

AS soon as a Pennine Way was first proposed in the 1930s members of the Ramblers' Association on Teesside were pressing for the creation of a similar long-distance route, the Cleveland Way. This would link up the old Hambleton Drove Road, the Cleveland escarpment and the coastal footpath. The first formal suggestion was made by the National Parks Commission to the North Riding County Council in September, 1953, and among the various other organisations and departments involved it took 16 years to get the route finally decided and officially opened at Helmsley Castle in May 1969.

Originally the path was referred to on the files as the "North York Moors and Yorkshire Coast Path". This is a description, not a name. Fortunately the more evocative title of Cleveland Way was eventually accepted. Parts of the route are alongside the political boundaries of Cleveland, but the Hambleton Drove Road was the ancient way into Cleveland; the path goes through the heart of Cleveland and it continues along the cliffs that gave Cleveland its name. Historically "Cleveland" stretched from Worsall to Whitby, the Lyke Wake route being its southern boundary for much of the way. Local Government reorganisation has made nonsense of ancient boundaries. Part of Cleveland is now, ridiculously, in Hambleton, and the present Cleveland County is only a part of the old Cleveland.

From Helmsley to Filey, by Sutton Bank, Osmotherley, Kildale, Saltburn, Whitby and Scarborough, the walk covers just over 100 miles. Compared with the Pennine Way it is circuitous. For a destination that is thirty miles east you begin by going ten miles west! The path meanders — but how magnificently it meanders — through the best of North East Yorkshire and three quarters of the way round the edge of the National Park.

For rich diversity of scenery — moor and sea, cliff and scar, hill land and woodland — there is no finer walk anywhere in the world and few areas have such a fascinating history. I have walked the Cleveland Way for over 50 years, but in traversing it again while preparing this book I felt more than ever, even in the dark months of winter, that richness and that fascination.

How to do the Walk

THIS 100 mile walk is one that is well worth lingering over. There is no time limit and no prize for speed. Arthur Puckrin (Lyke Wake Club) walked 90 miles to Scarborough in 18½ hours in August, 1962, but he did not often stop to admire the view. You are not likely to beat this record, so give yourself a week — or three week-ends. It would require great fitness to do the walk in four days of 20-28 miles each — Helmsley to Swainby; Swainby to Guisborough or Saltburn; Saltburn to Whitby, and Whitby to Filey. One of these on a long day would be enough for most people.

Sections of 8-22 miles are indicated in the detailed route for seven days. At least two of these should be split for a party wanting even easier walking — making nine days, or four or five weekends.

Shoes can never really be recommended even for this kind of walking. The mud is deep in places; sand can get into your shoes. Light fell-boots are best, with possibly baseball boots in summer. On both the moors and the cliffs the weather and the temperature can change suddenly. A drizzle at Clay Bank can be a blizzard on Botton Head. Always carry a warm sweater and a waterproof even in summer.

No-one should walk the moors and cliffs, even along pathways such as this, without some elementary instruction and practice in rock-climbing. Anyone with a bad head for heights should not do this walk. There is no danger on the path — but you are often only three feet from death. Walk always on moor and cliff as you should drive on the road — with complete concentration. In thick fog you would do better to spend the day at the nearest library or museum.

May and June are perhaps the best months for the coastal section, when broom and gorse and all the other cliff-side flowers are in full bloom. The moors are at their best from late August to early October — but autumn colouring makes this a magnificent walk till the very end of November. After that there is sometimes very good ski-ing on the Cleveland Hills!

Some (unofficial) figures show that, prior to 1974 Local Government reorganisation, there were 73 miles of this path under the NRCC of which 61 existed previously and 12 had to be negotiated.

Including Urban Districts there were 88 miles of footpath or bridleway (of which two miles at Kilburn and Roseberry have to be walked twice) and 10 miles of highway. Whitby and Scarborough towns add another six miles of street or promenade. This makes a total of 106, and it might be safer to add 10% for hills, ravines and other obstacles.

Walkers on the Way

FOR a great many years walkers have been doing the various sections of this route; few ever set out to follow it systematically from one end to the other. Alec and Alan Falconer had groups on the Hambletons, the Cleveland Escarpment and the coastal path in the 1930s. Maurice Sutherland, John Fleming, Tom and Florence Sharp, the artist Alec Wright and the archaeologist Frank Elgee are among others who must have done the whole of the route at one time or another. A good deal of it, Swainby to Whitby — was covered by a Cambridge University Yorkshire Society party in 1936. At Easter 1939 a second CUYS party (Joyce Reeve, Mary Dyson, Bill Cowley and others) walked from Byland to Rievaulx, Black Hambleton, Osmotherley, Bloworth, then through Farndale back to Helmsley.

In the early summer of that same year Mary Dyson and I walked the Kildale, Guisborough, Saltburn section (via Tocketts and Upleatham); the day after war was declared we set off with gas masks to Staithes and Whitby, then on to Bridlington, and finished along the Wold Gate. Two days later I received 24 hours' notice to sail for India and I did not see the moors, or Mary again for five years. In March, 1944, on the first day of a honeymoon Mary and I climbed up from Kilburn to the White Horse and were met on Roulston Scar by a hail of bullets. We then noticed a red flag was flying, and literally dropped down one of the slightly less precipitous gullies of the Scar. That nimble witch Abigail Craister could have done no better, and we did not rise again till we were a good three miles from the spot, above Gormire. After eighteen months in India and three Himalayan treks Mary died after a short illness in Simla.

Jean and Peggy Warren had done the southern part of the coast walk — from Bridlington — with Mary in 1935 and did the Cleveland Hills section with me on my return from India in 1947. After a fast climb up Botton Head Jean, in a weak moment, agreed to marry me and in 1948 we bought our first farm under Black Hambleton.

7

From 1969 to May 1987 just over 5,000 walkers had reported completion of the Cleveland Way taking various times from 3 days to 12 weekends. Probably as many more have not reported their walks to us.

The path is now well-marked in most places, but it is best to carry the North York Moors 1:25000 Outdoor Leisure Map, West and East Sections. They are rather bulky but are magnificently clear maps.

The Lyke Wake Club issues badges to and keeps careful statistics of those who complete the Lyke Wake Walk. It also issues circulars of up-to-date information on the Cleveland Way, and — although there is no time limit involved — has available a ruc-sack badge for the walk. Send requests for information to "Cleveland Way Secretary", Goulton Grange, Swainby, Northallerton, enclosing a stamped addressed envelope for reply. Reports of completing the walk should give just the dates and number of days taken, direction, any useful or interesting comments on route and details of accommodation. Send to the same address, with s.a.e. and 80p for ruc-sack badge.

The Lyke Wake Club also issues badges for the Shepherd's Round, a circular walk of 40 miles which covers part of the Hambleton and Cleveland Hills section of the Cleveland Way, linked by a route through Bransdale, Bilsdale and Helmsley.

Accommodation

SOME has been mentioned in the text, but details change so often that it is best to write to the North York Moors National Park Office, Bondgate, Helmsley, with s.a.e. for a Cleveland Way Accommodation List.

Camping has been reported at Wether Cote Farm, Cold Kirby; Hambleton Inn, High Paradise; Swainby (Blacksmiths Arms); Hinderwell;; Manor House Farm, Hawsker; Bent Rigg Farm, Ravenscar (Mr. White also has a hostel here); Burniston; Scalby; and Lebberston Cliff Camp Site.

Background of the Walk

Geology and archaeology

THE strata making the face of North East Yorkshire slope generally up towards the north, so that the older rocks come to the surface as you travel north and the north faces or scarps of all the hills are very steep. From Helmsley to Hambleton the upper rocks are mainly Corallian (Oolitic) Limestone. They have been referred to as "fossilised coral reefs". An interesting feature here are the "Windypits", fissures in Duncombe Park, near Antofts, behind Ashberry Farm, and elsewhere, in some of which beakers and flint implements have been found alongside charcoal of ash and hazel which gave a radio-carbon dating of 3,750 years. Natural underground reservoirs in this limestone are the basis of Ryedale water supplies.

The striking line of Tabular Hills marks the northern limit of this limestone, though pockets of limestone, as of coal, do occur in the lower and older strata that sweep up to the north. The peculiar whale-backed shape of the Tabular Hills — Easterside, Hawnby, Coombe Hill and Black Hambleton — is due to a hard layer of calcareous sandstone forming a protective cap over Oxford Clay, which has weathered to form the steep sides. Under this again is the Kelloways Rock. The great nabs thus formed stretch east to the coast at Scarborough.

The moors to the north, coming from under the Tabular Hills and sloping up to much greater heights, are formed of moor grit and fossilferous grit, on top of beds of yellow estuarine sandstone. Under these again are soft beds of Lias shales, which have washed away to make the steep-sided dales with their fertile bottoms. Where the dales come through the harder rocks and into the limestone at their southern end, they become narrow, wild and infertile, though high above them on the limestone plateaux are fertile fields and large farms, with more of a Wolds type of cultivation. Some of the arable fields on the Hambleton plateau are immense.

Between the sandstone and the lias is a narrow band of Dogger, which provided the Rosedale iron ore. There are also the Jet and Alum shales, which all round the dales have been extensively dug. The main bands of Cleveland ore were in the Lias, however — outcropping on the coast, where they were first found, and running too deep for economic working south of Kildale.

In the Great Ice Age glaciers swept down the Vale of York, over Cleveland and down the coast, damming up drainage channels, and forming various glacial lakes and over-flow channels. The Derwent, instead of reaching the North Sea at Scarborough, was forced through Forge Valley into the Pickering Lake and now has its outlet in the Humber. Eskdale and Scugdale were lakes. Boulder clay was deposited on the plains and morainic debris lay at the foot of the hills.

When early hunters roamed the moors between 7000 and 4000 B.C. the plains and valleys were marsh and jungle. Peat had not yet accumulated, and pollen analysis suggests that even the high moors were then well-wooded with birch and oak. Flint arrows — 'pygmy-flints" — have been and are still being found, always under or at the edge of the peat. The Mesolithic archers who used them must have been numerous, and the game plentiful. A lot have been found near the Drove Road, at Boltby Bank and N.W. of Black Hambleton.

The earliest convincing records of man in our area are from the eastern end of Lake Pickering. At Star Carr and neighbouring sites were hunting and fishing camp-sites of the Danish "Maglemose" culture, where mattock-heads of elk antler were found. Other sets of antlers were perforated for wearing by the hunter, linking up with horned dieties of the Celts. The Horn Dance of Abbot's Bromley has survived from a distant past. Radio-carbon tests give an age of 10,000 years for the Star Carr site. Was it the first of our Scandinavian invasions?

About 3000 B.C. came the first primitive farmers, with their stone and flint axes. One of their long barrows is on Kepwick Moor by the side of the Drove Road. The cremations connected with all the long barrow burials, and the broken character of the skulls, suggest a possible affinity with Aryan cultures of India.

The Beaker folk who followed, about 2000 B.C., and some of whose remains are found in the Windypits, also went up the Drove Road. One of their barrows near Hesketh Grange was excavated in 1864; it yielded three highly ornamented drinking cups. After surviving for 3,000 years these were destroyed by a German bomb (in

Leeds Museum) during the last war. Also found was the skeleton of a female with a jet necklace of 120 variously shaped beads.

The most numerous relics on our moors are of the Bronze Age, say from 1700 B.C. to 700 B.C., though all these cultures overlapped and flints were still being used in the Iron Age, which lasted through Roman times. The "Urn people" had settlement sites which can be traced in several places, often coinciding with modern dales farms. They left thousands of burial mounds on the moors; some of their stone fertility symbols are standing still — often, like their mounds, forming the line of present day boundaries. All over the moors are odd ditches, hollow ways, piles of stones, bits of old walling, stone circles and those phallic landmarks.

People wonder why there are so many "Crosses" on the high moors and whether religious ceremonies took place there. The answer is that many of the old stones were "taken over" by the church and new crosses placed where perhaps pagan rites had occurred, just as Rudston church was built next to the ancient monolith. We have it on Canon Atkinsons's authority *(Forty Years in a Moorland Parish),* that pagan superstitions still lingered on in Cleveland in the 19th century, while the 18th century folk lore of the Calvert MS. is most unchristian. The Lyke Wake dirge appears to be another example of Christianised paganism.

Descendants of the Urn folk must have been clinging on to hut sites such as that on Percy Cross Rigg above Kildale through British and Roman times. Roman remains have been found at each end of the Drove Road, at Cold Cam and at Whorlton, where a gold coin, bracelet, silver spoon and other coins were located. The Romans drove one main road over Wheeldale Moor to the coast, and they had forts at Huntcliff, Goldsborough, Ravenscar, Scarborough and Filey. Invaders from over the North Sea must have poured in unchecked after the Romans left, though it is obvious from the place-names that British pockets remained in isolated parts of the moors and dales into the 7th and 8th centuries.

There was a rich find from this period east of the Drove Road, at Sunny Bank above Hawnby, where a young Anglian lady of rank had been buried in a tumulus with all her ornaments. There was a leather girdle with a gold clasp, garnets and gold rivets. Her hair had been secured by gold and silver pins, and there were silver wire rings, blue glass beads, an iron knife, a stone spindle-whorl, and a decorated bronze hanging bowl, all from about 700 A.D.

In wondering about the past as we walk these moors I am sure we should think of life and culture, at any particular period, being more advanced than we might expect. At least in this small span of history men have not changed a great deal in themselves. They had the same kind of intelligence, and perhaps greater practical skills; even if they lacked our technology. For long periods the moors were probably less inhospitable than they are now, and there was not so much difference between the Urn folk's huts and the poorer Dales houses of the 18th and 19th centuries. Many an old farmer from the Cleveland Hills looks like a marauding Viking; another type, here and there, might have been left behind by the Brigantes.

Before that much-loved girl was buried on Sunny Bank, St. Hilda was ruling her Abbey of Whitby, and Caedmon (who may from his name have been a Briton) was singing of the glory of Creation from that cliff above the sea. By 787 Britain belonged so much to the English that they had forgotten they had come across the North Sea as invaders. In that year "first came three ships of the Northmen — the first Danish men that sought the land of the English race." The *Anglo-Saxon Chronicle* bewails the cruel ravages of the Vikings but it was "the Northmen" who were the pioneers of cultivation in many parts of Cleveland, and the majority of our place-names are theirs. The "wicks" and wykes" along the coast are part of their name, and the number of "by" endings in town and village names shows their influence.

Ubba the son of Ragnar landed with his raven banner — probably at what is now Ravenscar — in 866. It was in Cleveland that Harald Hardrada landed, before harrying Whitby, destroying Scarborough and going on to his defeat and death at Stamford Bridge. Possibly Scandinavian immigrants were coming in on this coast to re-colonise Cleveland after the harrying of the North by William. The Cleveland dialect is predominatly a Scandinavian language in origin. Thousands of words are still in use in the dales and the fishing villages which are more likely to be found in a dictionary of Old Norse or Danish than in any standard English Dictionary:

Rigg, a ridge or back;
syke, a small stream (or boggy place);
slack, a hollow in the moors;
grain, a branch (of valley or tree);
ling, heather;
stell, a ditch;
beck, a brook;
brig, a bridge or pier;
nab, a headland or projecting hill;
roke or *reeak*, a sea-mist or moor-mist.

These are a few which it is well to know. Even in 1987 you might meet an old man here and there in Cleveland who would disdain to speak English and would enjoy bewildering you with directions such as these, which were quite common in my own youth. "Lowp (jump) ower t'stell here, an gan up t'intak ti yon yat; there's a bit of a lonnin (lane) gans doon ti't'beck an ower a brigg; then gan stthrite up t'nab end o'yon moor, up bi that swidden (burnt patch) i t'ling. Gan ower t'rigg an doon thruff a bit of a slack inti t'gill. Gan up t'second grain ti t'reet — an yu'll ni reet!"

Knights and Monks

THE North Riding fought hard against the Conqueror. After the second rising William sent an avenging force north from York. Near Northallerton "so great a thickness of mists arose that men could hardly see those who stood by them, and they could by no means find the way." This sounds like a typical Cleveland sea-roke. If one comes down, it is just as well to get off the moors or the cliffs by a safe road and retire to some suitable hostelry till it lifts.

After the third rising William left not a single inhabited village between York and Durham, but a band of rebels formed a camp of refuge in Coatham Marshes. William came up in person, either by the Drove Road or by Bilsdale East Moor, to subdue them. On his way back he struck trouble on the Cleveland Hills, among "sharp ridges and deep valleys often filled with snow whilst neighbouring districts rejoice in the spring." It was the fiercest cold of winter, and for one night William was lost with six men. It is not long since a remark was recorded, made by a farmer below Botton Head, of someone "swearing like Billy Norman". The farmer knew only that "Billy Norman" was someone who had come over these moors a long time ago and kept himself warm by swearing!

Among local barons who forced Magna Carta on King John were de Ros of Helmsley, de Mowbray of Thirsk, de Brus of Skelton, and Richard de Percy. Immediately after signing John marched north with a Mercenary army, "satellites of Satan and servants of the devil", to punish these men, and Cleveland suffered again. Peter de Mauley of Mulgrave however was "one of the most vicious of the counsellors of John". In February 1216 John stayed for a week at Guisborough Priory, then went on to Skelton. Some of the opposing barons were placed in custody at Mulgrave, and John progressed triumphantly to Scarborough, thus completing a large part of the Cleveland Way. Only Helmsley Castle held out — but shortly afterwards John died and the Magna Carta barons were in the ascendancy.

In Henry III's time papal nominees were pushed into many English livings including Kirkleatham, which belonged to Sir Robert de Thweng of Kilton. Unable to obtain redress Sir Robert collected a band of friends and retainers, called himself Will Wither, and pillaged the property of Italian clergy anywhere between Trent and Tweed, filling his strong castle with rich spoils. Excommunicated, he went to Rome in person to protest to the Pope, who had to accept the justice of the plea. His grandson, Marmaduke de Thweng, saved the English army from destruction at Stirling by his great strength and bravery, cutting his way through the Scots and holding the bridge till the English could burn it. It was his niece Lucia whose "affairs" scandalised the Cleveland of her day. His son, Marmaduke, killed at Stirling, had been her first lover.

The North Yorkshire knights made up for their misdeeds by founding monasteries, and some of them ended their lives as monks. Walter Espec of Helmsley (who was succeeded by his nephew de Ros) distinguished himself at the Battle of the Standard in 1138 —

> Hys stature's large as the mountaine oake,
>   And eke as strong hys mighte:
> There's ne'ere a chief in alle the northe
>   Can dare with hym to fighte.

He founded Rievaulx in 1132 and retired there, to die in 1154. The third Abbot, Aelred, describes him as "a staunch and generous friend, of gigantic stature, with a voice like a trumpet, jet black hair and a long beard, a broad open brow and large, piercingly keen dark eyes." Roger de Mowbray was also at the Battle of the Standard, though not then 20. He founded Byland Abbey and ended his life as a monk there.

Another resident at Byland was Wymund, the piratical bishop of Man and the Isles. He had led his flock on marauding expeditions against the Scottish mainland for many years with success, but was finally captured and blinded. In the last years of his life, 1141–1151 at the Abbey, he would tell stirring tales of his battles, and describe the vengeance he would have extracted had his enemies left him "but the eyes of a sparrow".

The monks who founded Byland had themselves been driven out of Scotland with one wagon drawn by eight oxen. They first settled at Hood, under Sutton Bank, then at Byland, which became Old Byland when they insisted on calling their last and biggest abbey "Byland" although in fact it was at Wass. While at Old Byland the monks also had a chapel at Scawton to prevent "the divers perils and

14

fatigues which parishioners underwent in coming from Scawton to Byland." The "lesser bell" of Byland was conveyed "in a wain" to Scawton, but even so Rievaulx was only two miles away. "At every hour of the day and night the one convent could hear the bells of the other. This was unseemly, and could not in any way long be borne." So the Byland monks went first to Coxwold, then to Wass.

The Cistercians in particular were great farmers, and were the most important restorers of agriculture after the devastation caused by William. Rievaulx had granges and sheep-cotes in many parts of Bilsdale. The monks became tycoons in a very big way of business indeed, and their influence can still be traced in the agriculture of the area.

The abbeys of Rievaulx and Byland figure in another historical event — the Battle of Byland in 1322. Edward II had invaded the Lowlands, lost 10,000 men, and returned with "a single black bull". "By my faith," said Earl Warenne, "I never saw dearer beef." Edward crossed the Tees at Yarm and in all probability followed the Drove Road over Black Hambleton. Posting his men on a hill top he quartered himself on the monks of Byland, where he passed his time feasting and hunting, "minding more his own meat than the safety of his subjects".

The Scots under Bruce were in pursuit, burning some Cleveland towns and Northallerton as they came. On October 14th they attacked the English, in all probability where the glider station is established at Sutton Bank; they were repulsed by the English archers and by stones hurled down the steep banks. Some of the Scots then found an unguarded way up the hill, probably the gill called Scotch Corner, and rolled up the English flank. Edward was dining with the Abbot when the first fugitives arrived. On a swift horse he just managed to reach York and safety before a picked body of Scots caught up with him.

The Scots seized the crown jewels and the King's plate, stripped the monks even of their garments and took many prisoners back for ransom. However in 1346 the local knights — Mowbray, Percy, Neville and others — got their revenge. They routed the Scots at Neville's Cross in Durham, and thereafter Yorkshire suffered little from Scottish raids.

Huntsmen and Racehorses

The Helmsley Estate came from the de Ros family by marriage to the Manners family, Earls of Rutland, in 1508. In 1618 Katherine

Manners, one of the richest heiresses of her day, eloped with George Villiers, first Duke of Buckingham. Their child, the second Duke, gay favourite of Charles II, dramatist, duellist, wit and libertine, was also a keen huntsman. Retiring in disgrace in 1687 he took up residence at Helmsley Castle and spent the rest of his life hunting the fox with the farmers of Bilsdale.

The Bilsdale Hunt was never a fashionable one, but it is the oldest in England to have hunted the fox regularly. Stories of "t'Duke" were handed down for generations, so that he still seems a living memory amongst old Bilsdale hunting families. Spinks, Garbutts and Ainsleys had been in Bilsdale, some of them for centuries, before the Duke appeared. They have carried on the hunt as a farmers' pack ever since. One day the Bilsdale hunted a fox over the Hambletons and down into the country of a neighbouring, more aristocratic, pack. The fox went to earth, so they dug it out. The Master of the Hunt whose country they had invaded wrote a strong letter of protest and demanded an apology. There was no reply. He wrote in even stronger language about this ungentlemanly practice of digging out a fox in his country. Eventually he received a rather dirty postcard, written in pencil. "We allus dig. Nicholas Spink."

"T'Duke" set a fashion for hard riding. The Buckingham Stone by Tarn Hole Beck marks where the Duke's horse died under him after a three-hour hunt. There are stories of runs more recently which have carried on to the sea. Sometimes hounds went off after hares that turned out to be witches! The most famous character of all was probably Bobbie Dowson, who died in 1902, and whose hunting horn had come down to him from a forebear, Forster, who had been whip to the Duke. The "hunting" gravestone designed for him is outside the *Sun Inn,* Spout House, which for long periods has been the hunt's headquarters. The old inn, a cruck house, is of the 16th century. Bobbie once told Major Fairfax-Blakeborough (later the great Northern authority on hunting and racing) that he rode "like a cat on a darning needle".

The Hambletons were also famous for horse-racing. The name "Hesketh" comes from the Old Norse *Hestas skeith,* a racecourse, so Scandinavian settlers must have introduced the sport to these grassy uplands. There may have been racing there in Tudor times, and certainly by 1612 racing was an established event. For more than a century and a half Hambleton was the centre of northern racing, as Newmarket was for the South.

In 1724 Daniel Defoe noted that "at Hambleton Down near York are once a year very great races, appointed for the entertainment of the gentry and they are the more frequented because the King's

Plate of a hundred guineas is always run there, a gift designed to encourage the gentlemen to breed good horses." The "Plate" was in fact a gold cup which may have first been presented by the Stuarts. Queen Anne certainly gave this annual prize and the last she presented, in 1714, was sold at Christie's in 1933 for £1,473 — £57 an ounce.

However, Hambleton was hard to get to, and never had any amenities. Racing became more of a social function and after 1775 the "Hundred Guineas" race was transferred alternately to York and Richmond. A "Hambleton Stakes" is still run at York. The centuries old turf remained in use for training, having one of the longest straight gallops in the country, a distance of over three miles. But in the 1890s the landowner Sir Matthew Dodsworth developed some conscientious objection to racing and planted a belt of trees over the best gallop. Training went on nearby, and even Sir Matthew's moor was regularly invaded by strings of horses at daybreak before any of his staff were up. The training stables are full still, and many classic winners have had their final gallops here.

Sir Matthew Dodsworth was responsible for a good deal of afforestation on his estate. His forester was George Hartley, who lived to see the Scots pines from the gallop felled in 1938 and who was buried ten years later at Felixkirk in a coffin made from a Hambleton-grown tree of his own planting. He had planted a million trees from a nursery in Little Howldale, and he once had a poem published. The Hambleton Forest is now one of the Forestry Commission's administrative areas, with headquarters in Helmsley. About 18,000 acres are divided into seven Beats — Rievaulx, Scawton, Ampleforth, Hambleton, Osmotherley, Ingleby, and Guisborough.

Dorothy and William Wordsworth

Two famous visitors to the Drove Road and the Cleveland Way were the Wordsworths. On a hot July day in 1802 they set off with a sandwich to walk from Thirsk ("When the landlady understood that we were going to *walk* off, she threw out some saucy words in our hearing") to Sutton Bank, up the Drove Road to the Scawton turning, then to Rievaulx and Helmsley. Dorothy's journal is delightful. "We rested often and long before we reached the foot of the Hambleton Hills, and while we were climbing them, still oftener. I was footsore, the sun shone hot, the little Scotch cattle panted and tossed fretfully about. I could not walk quick so left

William sitting two or three times, and when he followed he took a sheep for me and then me for a sheep."

At Rievaulx "thrushes were singing, cattle feeding among green-grown hillocks about the ruins. I could have stayed in this solemn quiet spot till evening without a thought of moving. We walked upon Mr. Duncombe's terrace and looked down upon the Abbey, It stands in a larger valley, among a brotherhood of valleys — all woody, and running up into the hills in all directions. We reached Helmsley just at dusk." They went on to visit Mary Hutchinson near Scarborough, but in October they were back again, bringing Mary with them as Wiliam's newly wedded wife. "Helmsley stands very sweetly at the foot of the rising grounds of Duncombe Park, which is scattered over with tall woods; and, lifting itself above the common buildings of the town, stands Helmsley Castle, now a ruin, formerly inhabited by the gay Duke of Buckingham."

They stayed at the *Black Swan* and visited the castle, with its moats "grown into soft green cradles", also observing "There is one gateway exceedingly beautiful." They took a coach past "Duncombe House" and down the cart-track that the Cleveland Way follows to Rievaulx. After stopping on the bridge to admire the ruins "we walked up a long hill, the road carrying us up the cleft or valley with woody hills on each side. It was not dark evening when we passed the little publick house, but before we had crossed the Hambleton Hill, and reached the point overlooking Yorkshire, it was quite dark.

"We had not wanted, however, fair prospects before us, as we drove along the flat plain of the high hill. Far far below us, in the western sky, we saw shapes of castles, ruins amongst groves — a minster with its tower, minarets; a round Grecian Temple also; the colours of the sky of a bright grey, and the forms of a sober grey, with a dome. As we descended the hill there was no distinct view, but of a great space; only near us we saw the wild and (as people say) bottomless tarn in the hollow — seemingly to be made visible to us only by its own light, for all the hill about us was dark."

Wordsworth's poem was:-

> *Dark and more dark the shades of evening fell;—*
> *Yet did the glowing west with marvellous power*
> *Salute us; there stood Indian citadel,*
> *Temple of Greece, and Minster with its tower*
> *Substantially expressed—*

Dorothy was often a better poet than William.

Hobs and Witches

The Cleveland area is extremely rich in folklore which goes back to Scandinavian sources and often very much further. Perhaps the hobs, those strange hairy little men who did great deeds — sometimes mischievous, sometimes helpful — were in some way a memory of those ancient folk who lingered on in parts of the moors almost into historic times. In the years between 1814 and 1823 George Calvert gathered together stories still remembered by old people. He lists 23 "Hobmen that were commonly held to live hereabout", including the famous Farndale Hob, Hodge Hob of Bransdale, Hob of Tarn Hole, Dale Town Hob of Hawnby, and Hob of Hasty Bank. Even his list misses out others which are remembered, such as Hob Hole Hob of Runswick who was supposed to cure the whooping cough.

Calvert also gives a list of witches, "but they do be so great in number that mayhap it will show the more wisdom if mention be made only of those who in their day wrought some wondrous deed or whose word cast fear upon all." These numbered 21 and included Rachel Hesp of Carlton, Nanny Newgill of Broughton, Nan Garbutt of Great Ayton, Hester Mudd of Rosedale, Ann Allan of Ugthorpe, "Awd Bet Collet o' Sleights", Lyd Storm of Ruswarp, Susanna Price of Lythe and Leah Biggin of Stoup Brow. "And all these were at one time of great note — cast many an evil spell and charm, and were held in great fear by many good and peaceful folk. It be not for me to here put argument in the favour of what do now be doubted and scorned by some. I will but say that I have seen and know that which hath been wrought by these hags o' the broom, and of their power which they held at their beck and wink."

A story of the Hambletons was given to Calvert by "Robert Rymer, Cobbler, South Kilvington." Years before "there did live ower anenst Black Hambleton a witch-hag of great power and who did at divers times work marvels and wonders beyond the knowledge of the most wise. This witch-hag dwelt in a cave near the top of Black Hambleton. Her name was Abigail Craister. It does seem that by some gift or devil's device she held a great and wondrous power over both rattens and coneyes so that they did her will, and at one time the rattens to an uncountable number did work their way within the foundations of new buildings to the succour of a damsel there in secret hidden by a recreant priest with intent to ravish. Him they did worry the flesh from off his bones whilst the coneyes did work with so great a will that they did clear a hole to the bigness of a person creeping out. This dame to my thinking should on no

19

account be called a hag, she having to her credit a vast more of good works than ill deeds.

"Rymer did also tell me this. There was an old dame living in a cottage with her daughter an only child who had to her score more of beauty both of face and outward charms than many a one of noble birth. A young rake but the son of a good sire did long to have his will of her but she made him leave her in peace. It fell out on a day when she was gathering herbs for her mother on the moor he did come suddenly upon her but when he would have rudely forced her a sudden pain catched him in the eyes and he knew himself to be stricken blind, for black darkness without a moment's warning did come upon him. In mercy the maiden led him to his father's house — and later learnt it was to Abigail she was beholden for help at that time.

"The story doth end with a proper end up for we learn that the young spark did not long afterwards come to the maiden led by his own father to beg her to become his true wedded wife for no other way could his sight be restored to him so the twain had gained information from the wise man, one Kemp of Kilburn over anenst which place the damsel's home was, and they were wedded which to my figuring of it doth give a pleasing end to this matter. On another chance was this witch seen of several trusty folk to rise from White Stean on her broom and take for over Kilburn towards Coxwold. This witch dame could when need be turn herself into a hare or a black bitch the which there is good proof that she did."

I can only think that Abigail Craister had some early form of glider — and it behoves anyone walking along this stretch of the way to be particularly careful how they behave!

Jet, alum and iron.

Cleveland jet has been used as an ornament for 5,000 years. Its old centre, Whitby, is now experiencing a revival of demand. In the present century the industry has used mainly foreign jet, but the jet shale heaps along the cliff face and dale side in Cleveland show how extensive was the local search. This intensive mining occurred only during the 19th century, and probably did more damage to the dales from an agricultural point of view than the value of the jet found. "Jetting" upset springs and drainage, and spoiled many hard-won intakes quite apart from the unsightly heaps of shale it left everywhere along the 900 ft. contour, heaps which are still sterile after a century. It is extraordinary that landowners permitted this spoilation for what can have been a very small return to them.

It would seem that ownership of these open hillsides and moors was both less formal and less valued before iron royalties and shooting rights became important, and that many farmers and villagers just helped themselves. The extent of the workings also suggests what a surplus of labour there was in Cleveland early in the last century, and what a very great need was filled by the growth of ironstone mining and of Teesside industry. Jet occurred in irregular lumps and chance pockets at the bottom of the alum shales. Many of the "jet-holes" produced little or nothing.

The alum shales were worked in much larger enterprises, round particular centres where an alum house had been built. This was an organised industrial operation in contrast to the individual or group prospecting of the jet miners, who could sell their finds to buyers who came regularly from Whitby to such inns as the *Jet Miners'* at Broughton. Alum works existed at Osmotherley (Oakdale), Carlton Bank, several places round Guisborough (some of the oldest) and various coastal sites — Boulby, Kettleness, Lythe and Ravenscar in particular. John Chaloner (not Sir Thomas, of Guisborough, who usually gets the credit) played some part in introducing the alum industry to this country in the 16th century, but the popular story of smuggling Italian workmen away in wine casks and being cursed by the Pope is a much later fabrication repeated by too many antiquarians. The real, rather sordid history of this period is given in R. B. Turton's scholarly book *The Alum Farm* (Horne, Whitby, 1938). This early chemical industry was often badly run and the workers sadly exploited.

It was along the coast that Cleveland ironstone was first found in modern commercial quantities, though there was a blast furnace near Rievaulx producing a ton of pig iron a day in 1591. An acre of woodland gave 10 tons of charcoal which produced two tons of iron. The 1642 Helmsley Survey showed that 788 acres of woodland near the Rievaulx furnace had been stripped in the preceding 16 years. About a century later ore may have been brought from Robin Hood's Bay to a Durham furnace. Between 1815 and 1830 the Tyne Iron Co. were digging from the shore and working the cliffs in various places down the Cleveland coast. Later workings were carried on at Whitby, Kettleness and Staithes and the ore was called Whitby or Yorkshire Stone.

Blast furnaces had been built at Middlesbrough to utilise this long before the far better deposits near-by had been discovered, in 1849/50. In 1877 there were 39 mines working in Cleveland and

Middlesbrough had grown in half a century from two farmhouses and the remains of a monk's cell on the Tees mud-flats to a town of 55,000 with exports of well over £1,000,000 per annum. By 1915 Cleveland ironstone mining was on the decline. Pits began to close, as the best seams were worked out. The last pit, North Skelton, closed in 1964. I was down the pit that January day when the last holes were drilled in an ore face of the East Dip section 700 ft. below the ground, and the last truck was loaded with ore. Some piles of loose ore were left behind; I wondered for how many centuries they would lie there undisturbed.

All told, some 370 million tons of Cleveland ore went into Teesside in just over a century. Vast quantities still remain under the moors, but in uneconomic seams, for foreign ore can be landed by sea at a fraction of the cost of mining here.

Already by 1877 iron had revolutionised the social and economic life of Cleveland. The new opportunities for employment, the rapidly increasing markets for farm products, and the improvement of communications brought Cleveland in two decades out of the Middle Ages and into modern times.

Farming and fishing

In 1796, in his *Rural Economy of Yorkshire*, Marshall listed the main objects of Cleveland husbandry as "corn, butter, bacon, rearing cattle, and horses". He should have added cheese and flax. There were linen mills in various places and a sail-cloth mill at Hutton Rudby whose high quality sails were famous in far corners of the world. Twenty years before Marshall, Thomas and Emanuel Bowen published a map of North Yorkshire with the comment "Cleveland or Cliveland in the Clay, so call'd from the high Rocks and precipices with which the parts abound and Soil being of an exceeding clammy stiff Clay. Here is made very good Cheese, not inferior to that of Gloucestershire."

There still exist at Potto Hill — as on many Cleveland farms — four large sandstone blocks from a cheese-press. 683 carts and wagons, each carrying 25 cwts. of cheese, went into Yarm for the third day of the October Fair, the Cheese fair, in 1820. Only old men remember anything now about Cleveland cheese, because by the end of the 19th century Cleveland agriculture had moved from a subsistence to a cash economy based on liquid milk, beef, mutton and eggs, with butter only from the more distant areas.

Many Cleveland farmhouses were re-built or improved between

1890 and 1910, including both Potto Hill and Goulton Grange. The bricks for the new Goulton Grange were brought on the Scugdale (iron mine) branch railway. Another strange import back into Cleveland from Teesside was wagon load on wagon load of town scavengings (before water-borne sanitation was introduced) which helped to build up the fertility of many Cleveland fields.

Marshall was particularly impressed by Cleveland horses and by the road team of Cleveland — the three-horse cart. "The breed is strong, active, coloured coach horses. The Cleveland team treads the road evenly; and is the stiffest; the most handy; and for a level country and long journeys, perhaps, the most eligible team, that invention is capable of suggesting." He was referring to Cleveland Bays, which were famous as coach horses and are still used in the Royal Carriages. One well known breeder is Duel of Staithes, another is Sunley of Gerrick near Moorsholm. Horses have gone from the cliff-top and moor-edge fields to the Emperor of Japan and the President of Pakistan.

One strange fact recorded is that the late Sir Alfred Pease, of Pinchinthorpe, who published a Dialect Dictionary of the North Riding in 1928, remembered seeing a team of oxen in Saltburn about 1870. It had been driven down from Moorsholm, and must have been the last in Cleveland.

Nowadays the typical farm in the Cleveland plain is half milk, half corn, with a fair acreage of potatoes in some areas. There are of course some intensive pig and poultry units. An average size might be 120 acres, and 200 is large, though there are larger. In the dales of Cleveland the farm economy is often based on a moorland sheep-stray for anything from 50 to 500 ewes, though 100-150 would be the more usual number. The dale farm might be only 60-80 acres, with sheep rights (shared with others) over a thousand acres of moor. (By 1987 these numbers would be larger. Many farms have given up their sheep strays. On the plain there are fewer dairy herds, more corn and oilseed rape).

Fishermen as well as farmers have been affected by the industrial growth nearby. Staithes fish wives came to run their own stalls in the markets at Middlesbrough and Stockton. In the early years of this century over 50 cobles sailed from Staithes, and about the same number operated from each of Redcar, Whitby, Scarborough, Filey and Bridlington. There were 40 from Flamborough and a dozen each from Marske, Old Saltburn, Skinningrove, Runswick, Sandsend and Robin Hood's Bay. Wives and families worked late at night baiting lines or making crab and lobster pots. By the 1950s only a few were left the whole length of the coast. Even from

Staithes only one or two cobles went out regularly. Many fishermen went into other jobs — the iron mines or the ironworks — and did a bit of part-time fishing.

The 1960s saw a gallant revival. In many places, counting summer and part-time fishing, were more boats than ever — 70 at Redcar, 15 at Marske, 15 at Saltburn, 14 at Skinningrove. Runswick, Sandsend and Robin Hood's Bay are now completely holiday villages, but there are four cobles full-time fishing from Redcar, five from Staithes, 10 from Whitby, nine from Scarborough, 14 from Filey, four from Flamborough. The tractor revolutionised fishing almost as much as it revolutionised farming, as it enabled much bigger boats to be pushed into the sea. A modern 33 ft. coble, with echo-sounder, costs over £20,000. Other gear — nets, posts, van etc. — might cost a further £7,000. Few wives will bait lines now, and the fishermen either trawl or get old age pensioners to assist with baiting.

Previously lobster fishing was confined to the summer, to 10 fathom depth and two miles from the shore. The pots were liable to serious damage in a storm. The echo-sounder can pin-point rock ledges so that lobster pots can be shot accurately six miles out in 20-25 fathom where they are safe from storms. Lobster fishing, the most lucrative of all, can now go on all the year round. In 1971, with decreasing numbers of lobsters, some boats began salmon fishing with promising returns. The promise was not fulfilled. Now the licence alone costs £500 and the price of salmon has fallen. Unfortunately in 1987 prospects for in-shore fishing are gloomy. Costs have continued to soar, prices to remain static. To make a reasonable living and cover interest on capital, boats would have to earn £100 a day, with 150-200 days' fishing in the year, and this is practically impossible. Many have now given up — they love the life, but can get more money "on the dole". There seems to me to be a very strong case for some form of subsidy for in-shore fishermen, to enable them to go on fishing. The men who sail the modern cobles (with new names like *Moonraker,* or old ones like *Sea Witch* and *May Queen*) are amongst the finest you will meet anywhere, carrying on an old tradition — but how long can they continue?

The Drovers

The "Cleveland Road" or "Hambleton Street" was the Great North Road of England in pre-historic times. Romans and Normans used it. St. Cuthbert's body was probably carried along it from Crayke to Durham. It was used by priest and poet, by English and

Scottish kings and their armies, by an agricultural reformer (Arthur Young) and a church reformer (John Wesley, who preached at Potto and Osmotherley). The greatest traffic along it was that of the drovers. There are records of droving even in the 14th century. A York Castle deposition concerns a conspiracy to "take away the moneyes of James Walker of Hambleton, being in Scotland with an intention to buy beasts (being a drover)." Scottish and English drovers were mentioned at Malton in 1664.

The Act of Union with Scotland put long-distance droving on a firm basis, and for eastern markets this was the main road. Some traffic went by the low road through Harlsey, Ellerbeck and Borrowby, as the *Cat and Bagpipes* at East Harlsey suggests. (This really is the "Cateran Pipes", "cateran" being the Scottish term for drover). When the new turnpike was put through on the A.19 route via Jeater Houses in 1805, this was too expensive for the drovers and all came by Hambleton, so the peak years for the Hambleton drove road were probably 1805-1850, after which the railways began to take over the traffic.

From the Falkirk Tryst, and from Northumberland, droves of up to 400 cattle would be made up, and a "topsman" would go ahead to make arrangements for "stances" at every 10-14 miles. Limekiln House was one of them. The droving was mainly in late summer and early autumn; drovers would go from fair to fair on the way south. The cattle would be shod, and there is with one Swainby family a spare shoe of variable size, swivelling at the toe, that drovers carried. The drovers came to Yarm by Catkill Lonnin, Whinny Hill, Sandy Lees, Coatham Stob and Urlay Nook; from Yarm by Crathorne, Black Horse Lane (West of Potto and Swainby) onto Scarth Nick. An old stone farm-house at the corner on the main road here, Black Horse Farm, was the old drovers' inn before the licence was transferred to the present *Black Horse* in Swainby village.

From Sutton Bank drovers branched either to Malton or via Crayke to York for the Michaelmas and Martinmas Fairs. The old signposts on the Hambletons were to York and Malton and to Yarm, and the road is so indicated on an 1863 estate plan. The Kendall family used it as the normal way of driving sheep to Swainby sales till well into the 1930s.

Details of the Route

1. Helmsley to Kilburn — 10 miles.

The Cleveland Way may be started at either end, Helmsley or Filey, but I prefer the way that takes you into Cleveland by the old Hambleton drove road. Helmsley is a magnificent centre for walking. There is plenty of accommodation, including a youth hostel and several hotels (the *Black Swan,* a Trust House; the *Crown*; the *Feathers* and the *Feversham Arms* to mention only four). You could spend a week here alone, with a variety of fascinating walks luring you in every direction — to Elton Gill, Roppa, Baxtons, Bonfield Gill, Riccaldale and Skiplam — before you ever set foot on the Cleveland Way.

But when you do reach the Way, you might consider making Kilburn your first stage.

You might wish to spend an hour at Rievaulx Abbey. You could easily lose an hour in Nettledale watching a goldfinch feeding on some thistles, or seeing a scattering of coal-tits. You might surprise a fox on the steep hill-side — or a deer might surprise you. Then there are the training stables at Hambleton and the Gliding Club on Sutton Bank. Allow plenty of time for this section. Osmotherley is a dozen miles further on again and to do it in one day might mean missing too much of interest on the way.

The footpath to Rievaulx (local pronunciation "Rivis") starts on the other side of the stream from the church, keeping to the north of Robert de Ros's 13th century castle. Go up the lane past the new car park — the Cleveland Way is now well marked. After the fourth gate or stile it turns left down the hedge towards a wicket gate into Duncombe Park woods. Do not go through the gate, but turn right along the wood-edge.

The woods beyond the outside wall are lime, oak and horse-chestnut, with an occasional ash. At the other side of the steep little valley below are beech trees on Johnny York Bank. Presently you go down into this dip and immediately up the other side past an old war time camp. Between oak and beech you come out to a little lodge and a long terrace high above the Rye. The river winds below among flat alluvial fields, with wooded banks rising steeply for 500 or 600 feet onto Sproxton and Scawton Moors beyond. Typical of this area of oolitic limestone, the banks are split by equally steep-sided clefts and gills. Often they are twin gills with a narrow ridge between them, like Castle Gill and Antofts Gill, opposite you now. Here is a view to take your breath away. In autumn, when every slope is a riot of golden colour, you might think it is the finest you have ever seen. Along the length of the Cleveland Way there will be 20 other views as fine or even finer.

Pass south of the lodge, through a gate, and along a young plantation of beech, pine and larch which before long will block part of this wonderful view. Over a stile the track, which the Wordsworths once took, slants down past old limestone quarries to come out on the road below Abbot Hag Farm. (Hag means wood). Soon you will see the imposing ruins of Cistercian Rievaulx. In 1131 this was a place "of vast solitude and horror" where wild beasts abounded. It was the monks who drained Bilsdale, made roads, and created a flourishing agriculture. You pass an old canal which might have been used to carry stone to the Abbey, and signs of an old river bed, where perhaps the monks diverted the Rye to get more of the rich alluvial levels on their side of it.

Cross the Rye by the hump-back stone bridge, beyond which is a beautifully modernised cottage with sundial. A little further up the Scawton road is Ashberry Farm. One of the famous "Windy pits" is in the hill behind it. An old path used to go up the north side of the limestone stream from Ashberry, through thick woods and past clear pools but this is now a Nature Reserve. Keep on the Scawton road. At a cottage on the left a track goes off which is worth following on some other occasion. It is the "Monks' Trod" to Byland Abbey over Sturdy Rigg and Wass Moor.

Avoiding this temptation for the moment, go on past Hag Hall. Three hundred yards beyond this a double forestry gate on your right gives access to the forest road round Noddle Hill. Through birch and hazel you keep on in this general westerly direction, and presently the limestone stream is running close to the path. (Some artificial lakes have been made here, attracting wildfowl).

After half a mile there is a valley to the left, Bradley Howl. Take a sleeper bridge to the right over a little stream (there is a good bed of water-cress lower down) and go through the wicket gate to join another forestry road. This well-made limestone road goes right up the "Blind Side" of Nettledale and up Tankerdale through steep-sided fastnesses of elm, elder and sycamore where you may see rare birds and animals. About a quarter of a mile from the water-cress however you turn left off this at two big elm trees, along a green cart track up a side valley, Flassendale.

After about 300 yards turn right up another little side valley. The path goes steeply up to a grass field and a long lane that leads into Cold Kirby village, a place that seems to suit its name. If by any chance you have missed the path and gone straight up Nettledale to the Old Byland road, you can reach Cold Kirby by a path across the fields to your left, down a little dip and past a dew-pond.

The lane from Flassendale — Low Field Lane — comes into Cold Kirby on the south side of the church. Go on through the village and just before the Old Byland signpost, turn left down another cart track. This turns right, then left again, and in wet conditions can be a bleak and boring contrast to the warm luxuriant valleys you have come through. From the second corner keep south for a quarter of a mile till a forest track is reached. Turn west along this (Cote Moor) passing south of Hambleton House.

Hambleton House is one of those training establishments which made use of the bracing air and fine old turf of what is one of Britain's oldest race-tracks. Turn south and left here to the *Hambleton Hotel*, on the main road, highly recommended. A couple of hundred yards towards Thirsk, where a lane turns off south towards Oldstead, is a green notice "Yorkshire Gliding Club 900 yards". Behind it and bisecting the angle between the two roads, is the Castern Dyke. Follow this through the pinewoods and very shortly it brings you out onto the brow of Sutton Bank, and to a view which is worth any tribulations you may have gone through to get here. It is not the same view that anyone can see if they come by car. It is a view which you have earned and for which you have been prepared by the ten miles of walking that led you here.

Turn left along the rim of Roulston Scar, keeping the gliding station to your left. Knowlson's Drop, on the right, is where someone took the wrong path one night. It is a good mile round to the White Horse above Kilburn. This is not an ancient landmark. The village schoolmaster, with thirty helpers, cut it out in 1857. It is 314 ft. long and 228 ft. high, and was said to take six tons of lime to give it a white coat. It covers something like 2 acres — and 20 people can picnic on the grass patch that forms its eye. In recent years a restoration committee has raised over £3,000 to keep the horse in good trim. You are asked not to walk on the horse. The Thompson (mouse-sign) oak carving workshop in Kilburn is well worth a visit.

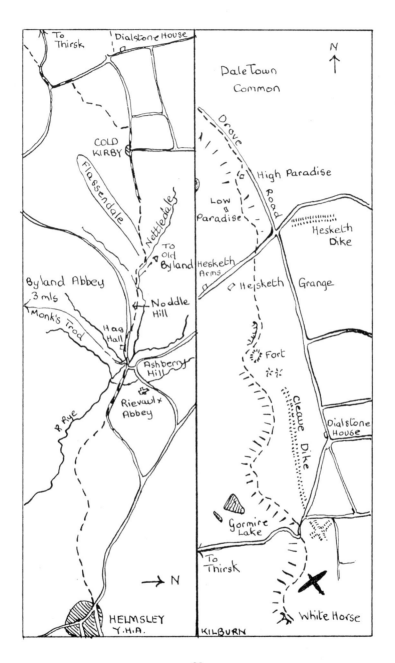

To Thirsk
Dialstone House

Dale Town Common

N ↑

COLD KIRBY

Flassendale

Drove Road

High Paradise

Low Paradise

Hesketh Dike

Nettledale

To Old Byland

Hesketh Arms

Hesketh

Hesketh Grange

Byland Abbey
3 mls

Monk's Trod

Noddle Hill

Hag Hall

Ashberry Hill

Fort

Cleave Dike

Dialstone House

R. Rye

Rievaulx Abbey

Gormire Lake

→ N

To Thirsk

HELMSLEY
Y.H.A.

KILBURN

White Horse

(Note: Kilburn village is not included in the official Cleveland Way route and you may turn north from the White Horse).

2.   Kilburn to Osmotherley — 14 miles.

From Kilburn you now head north into Cleveland. The drovers' road over Black Hambleton was a track long before the Romans came, and is certainly one of the oldest roads in England. It is metalled now as far as Sneck Yat, where the Boltby road comes over by Hesketh Grange and Hesketh Dyke. The footpath to follow for the first six miles is the one along the rim of the scars and cliffs. This joins the Drove Road at High Paradise Farm — and might well be called Six Miles to Paradise! Crossing the top of Sutton Bank, keeping west of the car park (where there is a National Park Centre and cafe) the path keeps to the dizzy edge of Sutton Brow, White Mare Crag and Whitestone Cliff, with Gormire Lake set like a jewel among the wooded banks some 700 ft. below.

The views are out of this world — and if you don't watch your step you will be too. Jagged ridges and sheer faces of limestone drop abruptly away from the path, and there is a sensation of flying. Many are the stories of horses who have taken their riders with them over the cliff, and one story of a witch (Abigail Craister) who "being hard pressed with hounds upon her track did from the cliff fling herself bodiley into Gormire Lake, and there sinking came not forth at that place but from a keld spring nine good miles from the lake."

Above Thirlby Bank, rim and path turn right-handed at a place called Jennett Well. There is a Nature Reserve here — but the well is now only a green hollow by the wall. Just before you reach this corner, at a tiny wood of dwarf larches, a path goes east to Dialstone Farm and Cold Kirby, along the edge of the training grounds, crossing the long line of Cleave Dyke on the way. For many miles this ancient earthwork runs between the drove road and the escarpment, curving slightly with the latter.

At the next corner of the escarpment, on Boltby Scar, is the site of a small promontory fort of the Iron Age. When it was excavated in 1938 a pair of basket-shaped gold ear-rings of the early Bronze Age were found under the ramparts, where they must have been lost for centuries before the fort was built. The fort is now only a grass-covered mound and ditch, immediately on your right as you pass through a new wooden wicket-gate, after the long curve of grassy rim that circles round Southwood Hall and its wooded banks below — a mile and a half perhaps from the "Well" to the "Fort".

Beyond the fort is one of the finest stretches of the whole rim. Dwarf larches are scattered on the wide grassy margin between cliff edge and cultivated field. The cliffs are again spectacular and at their feet is a chaos of fallen limestone blocks, bracken and scattered trees — a particularly colourful section in autumn. Presently you skirt — very carefully — a disused quarry with the foundation stones of what was once an aerial ropeway set in its flat grassy floor. In another few hundred yards you come to the wind-swept buildings of High Barn — an outlying part of Hesketh Grange just below.

The path now slants slightly away from the rim and from the Cleave Dyke across a long pasture to the Boltby Bank road just below the top of the bank. The Cleave Dyke can be seen where it crosses the road at the top of the bank, and at Sneck Yat crossroads can be seen the even more clearly marked cross-ridge earthwork, the Hesketh Dyke, with a stone wall going along its summit.

Your path goes straight across the road into a delightful forest ride between beech and larch, which brings you out above Low Paradise and right through the farmyard of High Paradise (accommodation). Another two hundred yards away from the rim and you are at last on the Drove Road proper. You have been separated from it for miles by from a quarter to half-mile of cultivated land, but when the Scottish and Northumbrian drovers used it for their cattle this was probably all open country, or at least much more of it would be available for grazing.

Striding north now along this ancient way, you come presently into the upper part of the great Boltby Forest, parts of which, planted in 1929, have already been felled. This pleasingly varied forest lies in a wide amphitheatre round the Thirsk reservoir below. There are alluring forest walks going off to the left, while over the moor to the right various tracks go back into Ryedale by Murton or Gowerdale or the Daletown ridge — every one of them magnificent walks through magnificent country. Just outside the wood on the open moor again is the stump of Steeple Cross, where a boundary line goes off in the same direction. You are climbing slightly all the way to 1,225 ft., past one of our very few North Riding long barrows to the left. A long gentle slope with exhilarating views along the vast ridge ahead leads to the Kepwick-Hawnby crossroad, and then to the ruins of Limekiln House.

Two tracks go down from here to Arden and Hawnby — one down the hill and one down Harker Yat ridge a few hundred yards to the north, past the next gate. This was a busy place once, with lime-burning and stone-quarrying, and the cattle-drovers passing. It looks desolate now, but I have met two people who lived and farmed here. From 1948-1951 I farmed not far away myself, at Over Silton. Opposite me in the tiny village lived Kit Cowton, then over 70 who as one of 10 or 11 children had moved down with his parents from Limekiln House to Hunter's Hill (in the Sorrow Beck valley immediately below Black Hambleton) about 1883. They had taken with them a goose sitting on a nest of eggs in a clothes basket.

Before them the Kendalls had lived at Limekiln House for a time before moving down Thoradale, then to Nab house just below. At Swainby sheep sale in 1952 I bought some lambs off Luke Kendall, who had the spare figure, the lean face and drooping moustache, of a Viking. His grandmother, Mary Kendall, had the last licence for Limekiln House issued in 1879. Tom Dennis of Nether Silton, who was 77 when he told me the story, in 1950, had known a previous licensee, Bob Wright. Bob and his wife used to go out dry-stone walling and leave their two lads to look after the inn — one to go down into the cellar and the other to watch the customer and not let him get away without paying! Tom Dennis had visited Limekiln House at the time of Queen Victoria's Jubilee in 1887, to light a Jubilee bonfire; they had drunk whisky there — but they had taken the bottle with them. By the time of the Diamond Jubilee ten years later Limekiln House was no longer inhabited.

Half-a-mile past Limekiln House the Drove Road veers left at White Gill Head above Whitestone Scar, though another track goes straight on over the Black Hambleton ridge and down by Bawderis Wood and Bawderis Intakes to the head of Ryedale. It seems probable that the place name here is in fact "Borderers", referring either to the drovers, or to earlier Scottish invasions. There is a Scotland Farm in Ryedale and a Scotland Nook near Solomon's Temple a couple of miles north on the Drove road.

From the high point of the Drove Road, 1,280 ft., the track is steeper and rougher down the side of Hambleton End. There is another magnificent view over the wild moors of Snilesworth and Whorlton to the Cleveland Hills, with the Cleveland Plain beyond. Eastward the moorland stretches for six miles or more, with few tracks. Even in recent years people have been dangerously lost here. Now, one of the last areas of remoteness in Britain has been spoiled by the erection of a thousand foot TV mast on the horizon of Bilsdale West Moor.

On your left as you descend, you see that the lower slopes of Black Hambleton have been afforested, though immediately below, near a patch of dark pines amongst the larches, some grass and stones mark the site of an old farmhouse, Swinestone Cliff. The

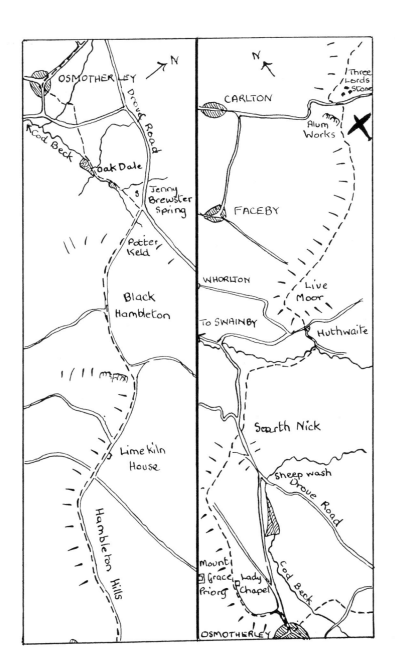

Above: Helmsley Castle, which has strong historical associations with much of the country traversed by the first part of the Cleveland Way. The 100-mile route starts near Helmsley church and passes to the north of the castle *(Arnold Kidson).*

Opposite, top: Rievaulx Abbey, as glimpsed from the 18th century terrace *(G. Bernard Wood).*
Bottom: The White Horse of Kilburn, one of the most prominent landmarks on the Cleveland Way *(John Edenbrow).*

Top: Sheepwash Beck above Osmotherley, just off the route of the Way at Scarth Nick *(Clifford Robinson)*.

Bottom: The approach to Skinningrove, a mining community much changed in recent years with the closure of the blast furnaces *(E. Cullis)*.

The Cleveland Way at Beast Cliff between Ravenscar and Scarborough
(Derek G. Widdicombe).

Inset: Roseberry Topping, the "Matterhorn of Cleveland" *(W.R. Mitchell).*

Top: Seaside donkeys take a rest alongside Whitby church and abbey. Cleveland Way walkers will do the same after climbing the 199 steps from the town below *(Clifford Robinson).*

Below: Landing a coble at Filey — end of the 100-mile Cleveland Way *(David Joy).*

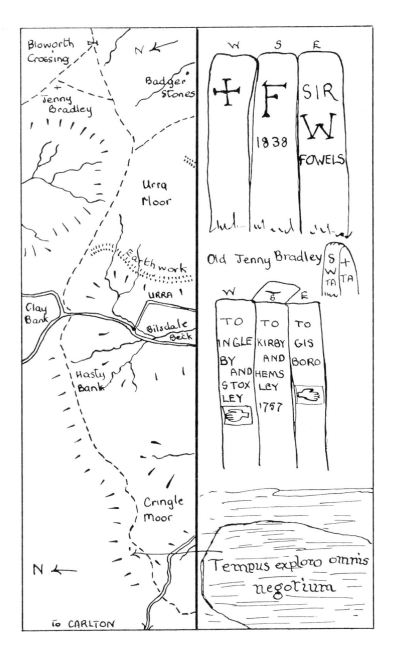

Bloworth
Crossing

Badger
Stones

Jenny
Bradley

Urra
Moor

Earthwork

Clay
Bank

URRA

Bilsdale
Beck

Hasty
Bank

Cringle
Moor

N

To CARLTON

W   S   E

F

1838

SIR
W

FOWELS

Old Jenny Bradley

S
W
TA

+
TA

W   S   E

TO
INGLE
BY
AND
STOX
LEY

TO
KIRBY
AND
HEMS
LEY
1757

TO
GIS
BORO

Tempus exploro omnis
negotium

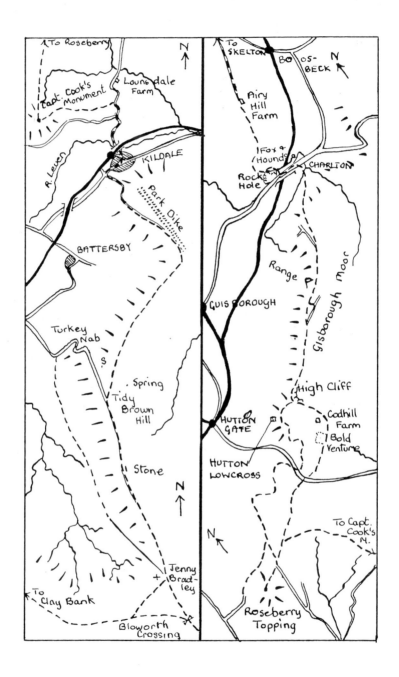

Dennis family are still farmers and joiners in Nether Silton, and some of their relatives are remembered to have lived at "Swinny" and to have made besoms — brooms of heather — for a living.

To the right of the path is presently a spring called Potter Keld (Potters are an old family in Thimbleby and Osmotherley). Just below are the remains of a fairly large limekiln or kilns, and then you reach the metalled moor road that comes up from Ryedale and goes on by Slapestones to Osmotherley. The Drove Road itself does not go into Osmotherley, but beyond Slapestones, once more unmetalled, it heads straight for Scarth Nick and Swainby. The *Chequers Inn* at Slapestones long ago gave up its licence and its century-old peat fire; its famous sign can still be seen:

> *Be not in haste — Step in and taste;*
> *Ale tomorrow for nothing*

That breezy Yorkshire writer A. J. Brown stayed here after coming up the Drove Road — and next day did the famous but difficult moorland crossing from here to the *Buck Inn* at Chop Gate in Bilsdale.

Your own path does not go to Chequers but down Oakdale to Osmotherley where there are three good inns with current licences. When you join the metalled road turn left over Jenny Brewster's Moor, which lies between Oakdale Head and Jenny Brewster's Gill. Was Jenny Brewster a local witch, an innkeeper's wife or an Osmotherley girl who met a Scottish drover on this moor? Nothing survives in local lore, but she must have been of some importance.

The path passes by a fenced-in spring which is also named after Jenny. It has an exceptionally strong flow, and has been piped in direct to the reservoir below. Aim for the junction of the two streams at the head of the reservoir, then your path is easy to find round the north side of it. A broad grassy path goes on down the next field to the derelict Oakdale House, above a second reservoir. The dale is lovely and you may see a heron fly off with slow heavy wing beats; you will certainly see a great many pheasants. A cart road goes up through a wood of larch, oak and sycamore and then across two grass fields to the road at Rose Cottage (recently rebuilt).

A few yards down the road to the left a narrow sunken lane turns sharp right. Follow this for about 250 yards. Through the third field to the left a track goes down to White House Farm. The footpath goes to the north side of the house, and down another field to a footbridge over the Cod Beck. Along this stream in the last century stood some linen weaving and bleaching mills; Walk Mill lower down was still working as a bleaching mill about 1920. The path goes up through Middlestye wood (stye or stee is an old dialect word for a ladder or a steep path) and across two small fields into the centre of Osmotherley village — the name comes from a Norse personal name, Asmundro.

The *Queen Catherine* (Osmotherley 209) has accommodation and provides meals. There are fairly good bus connections with North-allerton, and with Swainby/Stokesley/Teesside. There is a Youth Hostel in the converted mill building of Cote Ghyll (Osmotherley 575).

3. Osmotherley to Guisborough — 22 miles, perhaps 24.

Osmotherley's main street climbs up towards the moor by Rueberry Hill. As a boy of five I spent the winter of 1920-21 at Osmotherley for the good of my health — on doctor's orders. My health has never looked back since. It was a hard winter, and I remember vividly the mad toboggan run that set off from the top of the hill, right down through the village past the "Butter Cross" to the smithy below. Those were days when we would walk down to Clack Lane Ends to see the occasional motor car pass on the main road. My mother and I had come up in Charlie Barker's cart from Trenholme Bar station. Now not only the blacksmith but the station are things of the distant past.

Your own path turns off the road at the top of the bank, left up Rueberry Lane towards the Lady Chapel. Presently this forks, a newly improved track going to the right to the Lady Chapel itself, and the left fork going by Chapel Wood Farm. Both paths join again in Chapel Wood above the ruins of Mount Grace Priory. If you intend to make your next stage Guisborough, then unless you made a very early start you scarcely have time to make the short detour to the Priory itself, fascinating though this is. The only Carthusian house in Yorkshire, it was built between 1397 and 1440. Monks of this strict order lived here for 140 years in peaceful seclusion. Each had a two-story cell, with running water (from springs in the hillside above) and a private garden.

In spite of the austerity of their order, the monks readily accepted from Henry IV, in compensation for other revenues, "£100 per annum, and a tun of the better red Gascon wine." The Lady Chapel was built towards the end of the monks' period, probably 1515 — reputedly near their burial ground — and after the Dissolution the last prior, John Wilson, was allowed to retire to it with a pension of

£60 per annum — a very nice sum in those days. It is not recorded whether he also got the tun of Gascon wine! In the last century the Lady Chapel was restored, more or less as a cottage, by a Middlesbrough ironmaster, Sir Lowthian Bell, who had purchased the Arncliffe Estate. The family still farms the fields that lie round Mount Grace and under Arncliffe Woods.

Beyond Chapel Woods the Arncliffe banks have been re-afforested, and it is up a forest track (on the line of a much older one) that you now climb up towards the ridge. To your right is the quarry from which the stone for Mount Grace was cut; to your left, on the ridge, is a TV booster station, with just behind it Beacon Scar, a great rock used for long-distance signalling in medieval times. The path goes between the TV Station fence and the stone wall, and then round the rim with its magnificent views across the plain to the Pennines, and over Cleveland into Durham. To W.N.W. you may see what until the 1974 boundary changes was Yorkshire's highest mountain, Mickle Fell, 43 miles away. The peaks of Swaledale, Wensleydale and Nidderdale can be picked out as the eye sweeps round to the south.

Over the wall to the right you will presently see a white Ordnance Survey pillar. This — at 982 ft. — is the start of the Lyke Wake Walk, which goes for 40 miles straight across the high moors eastwards to the sea at Ravenscar. Your own route to Ravenscar will be much longer, but less rugged, and you do not have to cover it in 24 hours. For the next 12 miles, however, the path is the Lyke Wake path, and it is a well-trodden one.

Through a gate at the corner a well-worn track goes across Scarth Wood Moor. Below to the right is Osmotherley Reservoir, in the valley of the Cod Beck, through which you came yesterday. (Cod is from the British/Welsh word "Coed", a wood). Scarth Wood Moor has many prehistoric remains. Presently you cross the scooped line of a glacial overflow channel, and then you go steeply down into the much deeper one of Scarth Nick, gouged out along the line of a fault by the waters of the Scugdale Lake. This had been dammed up during the Great Ice Age by a glacier that covered Cleveland and reached right up the side of the hills, but never right over them.

Through Scarth Nick also comes the Drove Road from Slape-stones; it was here that Arthur Young, first secretary to the Board of Agriculture, commented on a journey that had brought him right along the Drove Road:- "It is melancholy to travel through such desolate land when it is so palpably capable of improvement — yet there are very beautiful prospects. You look between black hills down into extensive valleys. The most exquisite site is seen just before you go down into Swainby. After traversing a vast range of dreary waste, and shut up in a rocky hollow between two wild hills, you break at once on a view which cannot fail of astonishing. You look between the two hills upon an immense plain, comprehending almost all Cleveland, finely cultivated, the verdure beautiful, and the inclosures adding prodigiously to the view." That was written about 1770.

From the cattle-grid in Scarth Nick — where you will see an optimistic but inspiring signpost "Ravenscar 39 miles" — you cross an afforested section call "Coalmire", which means a cold, marshy place. There are jet workings, sandstone quarries and old limekilns around. The path slopes steeply left down an old shale tip, through a wicket gate, and in a few more yards turns left for a very short way to a gate and a green lane that goes on into Swainby village which you would take if you were making Swainby a stopping place instead of Osmotherley. Here it turns sharp right for a few yards down a hedge, then right again up the lovely valley of Scugdale. The stream is well below you as yet, and you are going on a good track between scattered oaks through a part of the valley that used to be a fenced rabbit warren.

Keep to the good path, well above a duck-pond, till you come to another wicket gate on the left from which the footpath slants across a field to the ford below Hollin Hill. Follow the road left to Huthwaite (or Heathwaite) where there is a telephone box. Apart from a tea hut on Clay Bank eight miles further on, this will be your last contact with civilisation until you reach Kildale — and Kildale's claim to civilisation is based on one tiny Post Office shop.

The path goes through the gate to the right of the phone box, towards the old shaft of the Marquis of Aislebury's Scugdale Iron Mine — which worked until the end of the last century (this area has recently been fenced and planted). You can see the line of the old ironstone railway across the field below the phone box. After a couple of hundred yards the path goes left through a wicket gate, keeping below the afforested banks, and over some old shale heaps. At the end of the plantation a sheep-drift goes steeply up the nose of "Knolls End" into Live Moor. Go straight up, and keep on across the peak of the moor. There is a cairn and flints have been found.

Below you to the south is the wild rocky valley of Snotterdale, with a miniature gorge, a waterfall and two deep caves from which coal was once cut. To the north the Cleveland scarp drops abruptly to the patchwork quilt of the plain. Between Swainby and Faceby is the rounded outlier Whorl Hill, which gives its name to the old castle and church of Whorlton immediately to its west. (Old Norse *hvirfill,* a round hill — and the parish is still Whorlton, not Swainby).

Through the 12th and 13th centuries the Meynells of Whorlton Castle were colourful characters. They held land along the coast as far south as Lythe. Stephen de Meynell was fined £5 in 1166 for appropriating a whale that had been cast ashore! They held lordship at one time of the manor of Yarm, with its ancient fair, and guarded the Drove Road, perhaps levying tribute on it, too. They held land at Hutton Rudby in return for serving the Archbishop of Canterbury, with his wine-cup at his enthronement.

Nicholas de Meynell, with Peter de Mauley of Mulgrave and William de Percy of Kildale "with red-headed John his groom to leads the hounds", on a poaching foray over these moors towards Pickering, "took 66 deer, and stuck the heads of nine on stakes in contempt of the Earl of Lancaster's keepers." For this escapade Meynell was fined 20 marks. However, when Edward II hunted the other way on in 1323 he was welcomed to a feast in Whorlton Castle and two local girls sang for him. Among local men who accompanied the Meynells on some of their expeditions are mentioned Robert de Pothau and John de Gauton.

Live Moor slopes down again to a path that comes over the col from Faceby, and just below the col on the north side, under a rock outcrop a few yards from the sunken path, is the spring of Copperty Keld.

The track goes on along the ridge to Carlton Moor, the entire surface of which has been bulldozed away to make a gliding club H.Q. To have two of these on one walk seems rather a lot. Gliders at least are silent, and soar like great eagles above the moor, but watch out for the launching tackle dropping as they take off. Just below, on Carlton Bank, the vast shale heaps which are a relic of old alum works are sometimes the noisy venue for motor-cycle trials.

At the other side of the road, beyond the Gliding Club gate, is a large stone. This, the Three Lords' Stone, is probably part of a tumulus, and marks the meeting point of three old estates — Helmsley, Whorlton and Busby. "M" on some of the old boundary stones stands for Manners, the family name of the Duke of Rutland, who held Helmsley and a large section of these moors for nine or ten generations till they passed by marriage to the Duke of Buckingham. They were bought from his trustees in 1695 by the Duncombes, who became Earls of Feversham.

A green path goes off from the stone past the Falconer memorial plantation, skirting a newly reclaimed intake, and climbing up onto the next great moor, Cringle, 1,427 ft. On the north face of

"Cringle", past the Hall Cliff Stone (where there is now a direction indicator, also a memorial to Alec Falconer) are several rock faces which have beautifully carved inscriptions on them, though the correctness of the Latin is sometimes in doubt. One is "John Coates" and others are "Amoris de Literatura - 1819". "Thomas Edmunds, Esq." and "John Rud, Esq." are very clearly dated 1732. "Rudd" is one of our most ancient words and names, going far back into unrecorded history. There is a Rud Stone on Urra Moor further along this route, and the very ancient Rudstone Monolith. There is a *Rudd Arms* at Marton in Cleveland and Rudds still farm and break in horses in the Stokesley area. Once they farmed Mossy Grange and Wildgoose Nest, deserted farms between Cod Beck and the Drove Road. On another rock face, incidentally, is "Tempus exploro omnis negotium" which might best be translated as "time solves all problems" — or might it be "I'll try anything once — and everything in time"?

The scarp on both sides of Carlton Bank has in places all the size and savagery of a Scottish corrie. Special care must be taken in darkness, fog or wet conditions. There is an alternative "Jet-miners' Path" round the face of the hills on the line of the old alum and jet shales, which outcrop everywhere around the 900 ft. contour. But generally the route across the peaks is to be preferred, though this will involve 2,000 ft. of climbing before you reach Clay Bank. The next moor ahead is Cold Moor, and this is almost straight up and down. A long ridge — "Cawdma Rigg" — runs south from here to Chop Gate in Bilsdale. On the col between Cringle and Cold Moors, where another very ancient track goes down to Kirby, is the stump of Donna Cross. In the west side of Cold Moor is another coal or jet level which provides a sheltering cave.

A forest track goes round the face of Cold Moor, and round Hasty Bank to Clay Bank. But you should not miss the climb up through the Wainstones onto the magnificent plateau of Hasty Bank. Again "hasty" comes from the Norse *hestas,* a horse, and one wonders whether here, as at Hambleton, those early moormen had horse races or horse fights. There are some good rock climbs round the Wainstones, "Rookery Nook, 45 ft., Difficult", "Milky Way, 35 ft., Very Difficult", "Sheep Walk Slab, 30 ft., Moderate", and "Little Bo-Peep, 35 ft. Severe (Strenuous)". The outside "Needle" itself is only Moderate, but the "Steeple Face", the cleft tower which is nearer to the summit rocks is "Very Severe in rubbers". There are other climbs further along, on Raven's Scar, including "Moby Dick", "Dirty Dick" and the 85 ft. (Moderate) "Tumble-down-Dick" on which my sons learned to climb before they were seven.

A 1642 *Perambulation of the Honour of Helmsley* describes the Estate boundary as going "from Haggs Gate–to Cliff Dyke–NW to a bounder called Birke Knott–W to Ravens Scar leavinge the Lordship of Broughton onN–W to Whinnstones and from thence to Pedlers Stone on the top of Broughton Browe–W to Couldemoore Ende–W to Donna Crosse on Kirby Browe–assendinge to the topp of Crindle Moore where the Beacon stoode leavinge Dromonby Lordshipp on the N–descendinge w-ward into a bounder called Hallcliff Stone on Broome Flatt Moore at Busby Browe Head–".

This boundary and Birk Knot lie at the foot of the crags where the hillside is all afforested, but presently you scramble down the NE corner of the scarp to the old boundary line at a point which must be Cliff Dyke, and then over a stile. Go down, between the forestry fence and the wall, to Clay Bank. The main road from Teesside and Stokesley to Helmsley, Pickering and Malton comes through here. If you go left along the road for a couple of hundred yards towards the big car-park at the top of Ingleby Bank (the lane which turns steeply off Clay Bank to Ingleby Greenhowe) you may be lucky enough to find a hut dispensing tea and other light refreshments.

The hill down to Broughton used once to be called Cushat Hill, "cushat" being a wood-pigeon. The old road however went much higher up and must have been a quite fearsome one. As a boy about 1930 I remember seeing the old triangular danger sign still standing forlornly on the hillside high above the new road.

In those days Ingleby Woods below, relics of a medieval deer park, were a glory of oak, birch, cherry and alder and the biggest concentration of bluebells I have ever seen anywhere. To wander there when bluebells were full out and the bird-cherry in full bloom was to walk the paths of Paradise, intoxicated by the heavily scented air. In the secret heart of the wood was a massive hollow oak which must have been a stalwart young tree when William the Conqueror was in these parts — and got lost on the moors above.

Twenty years ago all these banks were cleared and re-afforested, though bluebells and an odd bird-cherry here and there have survived. The old tree fell or was knocked down, and its great shell has now crumbled away, but I still remember the awe and fascination that gripped me on that magic day of Spring when, wandering through those scented glades, I first saw the gnarled trunk — and a brown owl flew silently away.

Across the road from the forest fence corner is Haggs Gate, and from it you begin the long climb up to the highest point on these North Yorkshire Moors — Botton Head on Urra Moor, 1,492 ft. From Haggs Gate a green track goes down at the side of the valley bottom towards Holme Farm, below the present road. That again is the old road, and the valley is a glacial over-flow channel. The main Bilsdale stream, the river Seph, does not come into it until just below Holme Farm, and you will pass the sources of the Seph high up on the ridge ahead.

Your path keeps up by the wall on your left, over a stile at the top side of the new intake and up through a steep narrow cleft in the rocks ahead. This is again a very ancient track. Higher up it is a paved causeway, the Sailors' or Smugglers' Trod. Smugglers certainly used it, but it probably antedated licensing laws by some centuries.

Presently you go through a wicket gate onto the open moor. On your left, behind a stone wall, are some dwarf larches that must have had a long slow struggle for existence against the winds that sweep over here. They have never noticeably altered in the 40 years I have known them, and they must have been at least a century old before that. If you have time, it is worth going south for a hundred yards or so from the larch trees till a rock outcrop suddenly falls away beneath your feet, giving a view of the Urra valley below and Bilsdale stretching away south.

It is another of the views that will take your breath away if you have not lost it all on the climb up. The wind sweeps up the valley and over this brow with incredible force — often it is impossible to stand on that rock and if you leaned out from the rock the wind would blow you back. "To get full expression of the very heart and meaning of wind," wrote John Ruskin, "there is no place like a Yorkshire moor. Scottish breezes are thinner, very bleak and piercing. If you lean on them they will let you fall, but one may rest against a Yorkshire breeze as one would on a quickset hedge."

Round the edge from above these rocks — you may follow it for a while before re-joining the main track — is a long and remarkable entrenchment. This crosses the valley below and keeps on right round the rim, past another rock outcrop called the Cheshire Stone and on for three or four miles to a point above William Beck Farm, beyond Chop Gate. Locally the system is called "Cromwell's trenches" but they are certainly older than that.

The name of the main ridge — Carr Ridge — suggests a Roman or earlier camp, and many have thought the trenches might be Bronze Age or British defences against later invaders. But a significant fact is that the upper part of Bilsdale belonged to Kirkham Priory whilst the moor here belonged to Rievaulx — the most probable explanation is that the trench was a monastic boundery.

On the main ridge now again you have Ingleby Botton dropping

48

away on your left. "Botton" is a Norse word for a wide steep-sided valley such as this. The springs that form the Seph are on the right. Soon you come out onto a jeep track or fire-break. A moor fire can be very disastrous, going deep down into the peat and destroying all the heather and a moor's carrying capacity for sheep and grouse. For the dales farms, a sheepstray may be their main source of income. If this goes they are lost. A terrible fire swept over Urra Moor in the mid-thirties, and as you will see in many places the heather is far from recovered yet.

Opposite the summit cairn — if you stand on the Survey pillar you will be just 1,500 ft. above sea level — is the carved "Hand Stone" mile-post dating from 1711, and the possibly Celtic Face Stone further on. The 1642 "Perambulation" already quoted mentions the latter "Forward to Bagerstone leavinge Cockinge Rigg (beinge the land of Lorde Duke of Buckingham) on E–N–warde up Barney Gill to the Streete Way–NW to the bounder called Faceston leavinge Greena Button on the NE–So to the bounder called Button Hoe."

The Badger Stone is a huge rock shaped like a badger's head; it stands just over a quarter of a mile south, above the Hodge Beck that forms one of the two heads of Bransdale. Cockayne Ridge lies between the two. Another ancient track, long lost in heather, comes up from Helmsley by the Badger Stone and joins the "Streete way" at the Rud or Red Stone, which is just after a bend in the fire-break round a marshy spot. The paved causeway must in 1642 have gone much further down towards Haggs Gate. I have heard that Bilsdale farmers took some away for their farmyards. Others were used to make shooting butts. Lengths of the old causeway can be seen on the left of the fire-break.

The other track was called "Thurkilstye" and this in fact is the one you are now going to follow, though for a few hundred yards they coincide. The Street way or Smugglers' Trod goes on to Rudland Rigg about where the Rosedale ironstone railway comes over at Bloworth level crossing. Parts of it can be found just to the south of the track. It may have gone on into Farndale or just linked up with the Rudland Rigg road. So far no paved causeway has been found beyond here.

The Lyke Wake Walk takes the route east to the sea along the obvious line at this point of the railway itself. Your own path now turns north along Rudland Rigg, but instead of keeping on to Bloworth, from the dip beyond Rudstone (which is Bloworth Slack and forms the other head of Bransdale) you can turn left up another fire-break and then follow the old line along towards Incline Top. Here the ore went down to the main line below. The engine shed still stood up here, a prominent landmark, during the 1930s. There are people living who rode on the empty ore-wagons back to Blakey or Rosedale. The line was still working in 1920 but was finally taken up in 1928.

On your left before you reach Incline Top is Rud Scar, site of the Greenhowe ironstone mine, or rather quarry. There is a chaos of old workings round here. A landmark to your right is "Jenny Bradley". Make for this and you will be on the hard road north towards Battersby. There are two stones at "Jenny Bradley". The smaller and older one is indecipherable now. The taller one has SIR W FOWELS deeply cut on the north side: F 1838 on the south, and a fine cross, with what looks like T A 1768 on the west.

The stone marks the beginning of the Ingleby Estate which was given to Guy de Baliol by William II. After going to the Eures by marriage it was bought in 1609 by David Foulis, a Scotsman who came with James I to England. Sir William Foulis was the 8th baronet. He died in 1845; a daughter took the estate in marriage to the Sidneys, Lords De L'Isle and Dudley. There is no record of who Jenny Bradley was but she had a sister, Margery Bradley (or "Old Margery") a large, rough, Celtic looking stone on Blakey Rigg, a miile south of Ralph Cross. There is a similar stone, the "Cammon Stone", a mile and a half south of Jenny, on Rudland Rigg.

As you walk north along Rudland Rigg, Ingleby Botton, with its farms and wooded stream, is below you on your left, and beyond it the hills you have just walked over jut above the Cleveland Plain, like lions ready to spring. The hill next on your right, with another old stone in the tumulus on top, is Botton Howe. A mile over open moor to the east is the beautiful little valley of Grain Beck, running parallel to Rudland Rigg and ultimately curving east to form Baysdale. In it are the ruins and old intakes of Grain House. Where it turns east stands Baysdale Abbey, now just a farmhouse with some stone work and a fine old bridge (rapidly disintegrating) from the monastic period.

The small nunnery had originally been founded at Hutton Low Cross near Guisborough in 1162. This later moved to what is now Nunthorpe and then to Baysdale. We know that one of the Prioresses was called Susanna, that there was traffic between Rosedale and Baysdale Abbeys, and that the Abbey was finally closed down because of alleged dissolute behaviour.

There are traces of another flagged road on Middle Head moor, and a curious jumble of rocks called the Cheesestones. On the far side of Grain Beck, Stony Ridge, Stockdale and Great Hograh Moors sweep over into Westerdale. Many interesting archaeological finds have been made there.

On the north side of Botton Howe there are many stones lying around which invite curiosity, and about a mile north is another finely carved stone which has weathered very well. It has a hollow on top — perhaps, like Ralph Cross, intended for the leaving of alms — and on the south side are hands pointing "To Ingleby and Stoxley" and "To Gisboro".

The valley dropping down behind the stone is that of Black Beck, the other main tributary of Baysdale; along the ridge to the left, at the other side of Baysdale Farm, you can see two miles away part of the metalled road on Park Nab along which your path goes. If you would like a stretch of heather and bog-wallowing you could indeed strike down to the left of Black Beck aiming for the top intake wall in Baysdale. There is an old stone ruck halfway, a pile or pillar of loose stones, which occur much less frequently on the moors than the single standing stones, and have an even more obscure origin.

If you keep on in the Ingleby-Battersby direction, however, you pass some curious rock outcrops on the left, and find another old milestone marked "Greeno Road". On your right now is the rise called "Tidy Brown Hill". "Brown" is almost always found applied to a rounded hill and, since the hills are no browner than the rest of the moor, probably comes from the British/Welsh *bron,* a breast; "Tidy" or "Tiddy" meaning little (c/f Tidkin Howe).

In another hundred yards or so there is an iron gate across a track to the right, with a wooden wicket gate beside it. A newly cleared track goes straight along for Baysdale head and Park Nab and here you leave the Rudland Rigg road just before it drops down Turkey Nab to Battersby and Ingleby Greenhowe. There is, however, a very fine Saxon and Norman church in Ingleby and an excellent inn, the *Dudley Arms.* No other inn will be seen before Guisborough.

It was a Bransdale man (a Strickland) when Vicar at Ingleby who was responsible for some of the Latin, Greek and Hebrew inscriptions that can be found in places between here and Bransdale — e.g. on the Cammon Stone. "Turkey" is a corruption of Thorkill, the Norse settler who gave this stretch of track its name.

The track for Park Nab slopes down now between two of the Three Sisters (springs). The ridge between Baysdale and Battersby narrows, and soon you are on the metalled road. Presently there is a gate, "Juniper Gate", and on the right just before this is a small tumulus called "John o' Man's Cross". No sign of a cross exists, and only the name is of interest. A few yards beyond the gate a very old wall, built on a mound above a ditch, comes up from below and runs alongside the road. Although the road is the official path for the next mile or so into Kildale, it has nothing of note along it except that just below it, a few hundred yards from the next corner, is a peculiar large stone looking rather like an altar. In fact, it is a millstone that someone — centuries ago perhaps — has tried to carve out, and hasn't quite finished. It is worth following the old wall "Park Dyke" on from the corner onto the top of the ridge.

Down to your right is the source of the river Leven, which curves round back through Kildale. It is the last — and the longest — of the tributaries of the river Tees, and like it bears a Celtic name. "Leuan" is a Welsh water-nymph. The chimney of the old Warren Moor iron mine, which was not a very successful one, can be seen down Kempdale, as the head of the Leven is called. The moor on the far side is called Kempswithen towards its eastern end, another fascinating place name "Swithen" or "swidden" was the Old Norse term for burning-off the heather and clearing the moor, and is still used locally for the regular rotational burning-off of over-long heather. Kempswithen, incidentally, was the subject of an 18th century attempt at moorland reclamation by Sir Charles Turner of Kildale which was a little too ambitious. The heather soon crept back.

The whole area is full of prehistoric remains which have fascinated archaeologists for a century and which will continue to yield their slow story. The Park Dyke is almost certainly medieval. Some of the large stones that form its base have markings on them. If you walk along with the wall to your left you will find several of these. R C and T occur, the latter probably for Turner. There are Hs and a double W. These could all be later additions. There is at least one stone with a cup and ring marking, like a Scout's "Gone Home" sign. This mark, fairly frequent elsewhere, is still a mystery. It could represent a barrow with a surrounding dyke — or it could be some prehistoric game of marbles! Along the ridge of Park Nab itself is another and probably much more ancient earthwork. Archaeological finds will probably be made here some day as there are interesting groups of stones.

It had been hoped that a path could be opened along the line of the Dyke direct into Kildale village. However it is very little further to drop down from the Nab to the road. The sheer rocks here have some more climbs on them, but be careful. There has been one fatality here. In Kildale village there is a post office shop and a church; the latter, rebuilt in 1868, has a few Saxon stones outside the porch. Behind it is the site of the moated medieval manor. This belonged to the Percy family and was their chief residence until they acquired Alnwick in 1309. Two of them who fought in the Crusades are buried here, and the moor to the NE is Percy Cross Rigg. John Turner of Kirkleatham bought the estate from the Percy family in 1660.

The path goes along the road to the right (under the railway) marked "No through road for motors". After crossing the Leven you will notice some marshy land on the left. Here were two fish ponds, and the remains of the dam can be seen at the wood corner where the road turns up the hill. In July 1840 there was a great flood which swept dam and ponds away. A 30 ft. wall of water went down the gorge beyond, destroying an old corn mill and damaging the Bleach Mill a mile away. No lives were lost.

You have now an embarrassing choice of paths — the low, the middle, or the high. One goes along the right bank of the stream, past a waterfall called Old Meggison. You then climb up to the right either through Mill Bank Wood or Bleach Mill Intake onto Easby Moor. Another main track goes through the wood more or less on a countour from the next corner of the road below Bankside Farm. This goes round the nab of Easby Moor, and a branch links it with the top path.

The top path is the designated and the finest one. It does necessitate going on up the road to the summit of the hill, at Pale End Plantation, where a forest road goes left along the ridge.

If you are in a hurry to reach Guisborough you can go straight on from Lounsdale onto Percy Cross Rigg and north along another fine track to Hutton Gate. The detour by Captain Cook's monument and Roseberry Topping, is one that nobody would wish to miss. The forest track from Pale End ("The Pale" was probably a hunting enclosure of the Percy family) heads straight along the ridge of Coate Moor for the Monument. At some gate-posts keep to the grass track through a larch wood to the left of the main forest track. Keep to the rim of the ridge and you will get the best views. Just below the rim are two huge old beech trees, with other beech and oak below. Some of the new planting is mixed beech and pine.

There are some rock outcrops forming a little amphitheatre below, and the track slopes up to the Monument to "the celebrated circumnavigator Capt. James Cook, F.R.S. A man in nautical knowledge inferior to none, in zeal, prudence and energy superior to most." This was placed here by Robert Campion of Whitby in 1827. Many beacon-fires and celebratory bonfires have also been lit at this spot. There has certainly been no greater Yorkshireman than James Cook. A farm worker's son from Marton, who went to school at Ayton, his country was the plain you see below. The seas of the world were his conquest. For an 18th century farm labourer's son to become a Captain in the Royal Navy and a Fellow of the Royal Society would be sufficient to mark him as an extraordinary character, yet these were only a token of his real achievements. From Easby Moor you can see in imagination Australia and New Zealand and all the scattered islands of the vast Pacific.

From the monument a broad track heads north above Hunter's Scar and down the side of Cockshaw Hill to Gribdale Gate. Over the cattle grid the road enters Lounsdale. In descending you cross the line of the Whinstone Ridge, a narrow dyke of basalt which is the result of some ancient volcanic eruption and which stretches from the Tees right across Cleveland to the coast near Ravenscar. Where it has been quarried out for road metal, as in the Langbaurgh Ridge below Roseberry (which gives the Langbaurgh Wapentake of Cleveland its name), the result is a canyon like a railway cutting. All round here are old ironstone mines and quarries. Time has cloaked these industrial workings better than it has the alum shales.

From the cattle grid a footpath goes directly up the ridge opposite, past a scattering of pine trees above Summer Hill. A quarter of a mile over the moor to the right, apart from various scattered tumuli, there is one tumulus with a large oval enclosure in front of it. This has been excavated and found to be Neolithic with the enclosure later Iron Age. Pollen analysis revealed that when the cairn was built there was mixed forest round, with traces of initial clearance (5000-2000 B.C.). By the time of the enclosure the site was treeless and cultivation was in progress (600 B.C.). Cultivation of the moor here was at its peak in the Iron Age after 600 B.C. Only after the Iron Age did the heather spread.

From Newton Moor you must turn west for half-a-mile to climb Roseberry Topping, the Matterhorn of Cleveland, whose S.W. face slid away in 1907 because of iron-mining subsidence below. According to an 18th century play, Margery Moorpoot, Roseberry "is t'highest hill i all Cleveland, aboon a mile an a hawf high, an snaw on t'top i t'hottest day i summer". Actually it is 1,057 ft., seven feet less than Easby Moor. The hill was the Viking's "Odinsberg" — Othensberg in 1119 — then Ouesbergh. The village below was Newton under Ouesbergh but by a process of metanalysis the "r" was added to the hill, the village became Newton under Roseberry and so the hill got its present name. The view is magnificent, with a great arc of sea to the North and North-East. There is a good inn, the *King's Head*, in the village, half a mile away and 720 ft. below.

There is an old legend of a Saxon prince whose death by drowning was foretold. His mother brought him to the top of Roseberry for safety, but on the saddle below the peak was a well. In it, sure enough, he was drowned!

Retracing your steps past the site of this well — no more now than a few clumps of rushes — you climb up again to a gate, at the corner of two walls, through which you came previously. Instead of following the wall to the right back onto Newton Moor, or the wall to the left onto Pinchinthorpe Moor, bisect the angle and head due east or slightly north of east onto Hutton Moor. There are several tumuli, and several boundary stones, that will attract your interest. One is marked TKS 1815 — the Lord of the manor of Newton at that time was Thomas K. Staveley, of Ripon. Another stone is dated 1752. A T alone may stand for Turner (now Turton), whose land comes up on the Kildale side.

The path proper keeps to the north of the boundary stones, and then as you descend towards the rough Hutton Gate-Percy Cross Rigg road you should keep to the south of a small clump of spruce, a 1935 trial planting which has been already outgrown by some tress of a 1950 planting in the main afforestation a few hundred yards to the north. Cross the rough road and keep on the heather just above the bracken, aiming for the boundary wall along the intakes south of Codhill Farm. This is usally called Highcliff farm, but the old name, which was the original name of Hutton Lowcross village below, probably comes from the Welsh "coed", wood.

Keep between the main bracken bed below, and a small bracken and rush patch above, and you will pick up a good track. There is a stone — TC G 1860, probably Thomas Chaloner, of the Guisborough Estate. The path crosses a woodlined water-course, which until recently carried the water supply for Hutton Lowcross down to a filter house below. The big intake just beyond is called "Bold Venture" on the 2½″ map. It is said to have first been cultivated from rough grazing by the tenant of Codhill Farm, Wedgewood, at the beginning of the century. He called it his "Golden venture". However J. W. Ord refers to "Bold Adventure Gill" prior to 1850. To win this back from the moor, even to rough grazing, must have been a very bold venture by the man who first did it.

The Wedgewood who carried on the improving process emigrated to Canada. The present occupier of Cod hill Farm is George Humphreys, who has been there 44 years. He was ploughing Bold Venture when I checked this section. It was a late November day, with a wind blowing straight from the North Sea. "A cold day for ploughing," I said. "Aye," replied George, "but I'm not complaining." What he apparently liked least was tramping round these moors after his 200 sheep.

Your path keeps along outside the intake wall — and parts are very boggy. At the far end of the last intake past the farmhouse, a wicket gate goes through into a wood on your left. If in fact you kept straight on you would come out onto the moor edge above Guisborough where you want to be, but you would miss Highcliff itself. Turn into the wood, then at the second wicket gate, turn right along a path between larch tress on the left and pine on the right. Cross a forest road and this path climbs right up to the imposing cliff itself. There are more rock-climbs here and also a cross carved, ominously perhaps, at the foot of one rock face. Climb up on the right side and make your way along the rim till you come out on the forest road again, heading slightly north of east.

A very pleasant alternative to all this from Roseberry is to slant down from the saddle below Roseberry or, if you have succumbed to the temptation of the *King's Head,* then keep along the bridle path which goes off left from the wood at the top of the lane, making for the forest road that goes right round the face of the hill more or less on a contour a couple of hundred feet below the Hanging Stone. Keep to the right round the head of Bousdale and in another half mile you come to the Percy Cross road again just past a Forestry Commission hut. Keep straight on across the cart-road into "Bold Adventure Gill" past the filtering tanks, then where the main forest road turns down for Hutton Lowcross take the road to the right which goes past shale heaps from the old Hutton mine.

This mine yielded over 200,000 tones of ore a year for about 20 years from its opening in 1852. A very rich jet seam was worked here at one time. There is a turning to Highcliff Farm (Codhill) but keep on till the main forest road starts to descend. A right turn here takes you up to Highcliff. This alternative is slightly longer, but better and faster going. It goes through some of the finest afforestation I have seen. It is imaginative planting, with small irregular blocks of many different tress blending in with the steep and broken hillsides and hiding the scars of old industrial workings. There are clumps of cypress, stands of hardwoods and a few patches of old natural scrub left here and there as contrast.

For anyone intending to stay in Guisborough it is probably best to leave Highcliff until morning and go straight down through Hutton Lowcross to Hutton Gate.

About an hour further on from Highcliff, and right by the side of your path, is the *Fox and Hounds Inn,* Slapewath, which has a restaurant and accommodation (0287 32964).

4. Guisborough to Saltburn — 8 miles (from Hutton Gate).

This is a short section, which can be done in a morning but allow four hours to be on the safe side. It is the least pleasant, as it goes through the heart of the East Cleveland ironstone mining district. For the first hour you circle round Guisborough along forest tracks at the edge of Gisborough Moor. The Moor, like the Lord, drops the "u".

The town is spread below you and the Priory ruins, with their one imposing arch, can be clearly seen. This, the most important Augustinian Priory in Yorkshire, was founded by Robert de Brus about 1120. On May 16th, 1289, the church was burned down when a "vile plumber" left his fire burning in the roof when repairing the lead. The ruins you see are of the church built in 1309.

The Bruces — one branch of this great Cleveland family became the Scottish kings — gave the Priory "all Guisborough with all things pertaining to it" and most of the land you can see from the ridge — Kirkleatham and Coatham, the churches of Marske, Skelton, Danby and Upleatham among others, in addition to 2,000 acres of cultivated land and 8,000 acres of common and moor. The monks of Guisborough were not free from faults, however. After an Archbishop's visitation they were forbidden to go out of the Priory after Compline "for the sake of drinking", while the canons were bidden to listen to edifying discourses instead of improper tales. In a sense the Prior and Canons of Guisborough were pioneers of the Cleveland iron trade, for early in the 13th century they had forges in Glaisdale.

As you travel east through the new forests towards Slapewath you pass over one after the other of the later Cleveland ironstone mines — Hutton, Belmont, South Belmont, Spa Wood and Slapewath — with many more beyond. The forest roads are something of a maze, and will be worse when the trees have another five years' growth on them, but somewhere above Belmont you take a left fork. The path comes out of thick forest on a left-hand turn, and turns right along the edge of open fields, with the steep wooded scarp above Old Park Farm on your left. Four minutes along here a wicket gate on your right takes you onto an old stone track through a grass field with oak trees. This leads very shortly to a gate and a concrete roadway sloping down left-handed. Two or three minutes down here, at some gate-posts, the path leaves the road over a stile to the right. Soon you are going through woods and over cleared slag tips (with uncleared ones towering above you) and almost parallel to the main road. You can see the Fox and Hounds to your left but you have to keep on through the wood and onto a farm track which slants down left to the road near Charltons. Turn left on the lay-by to reach the Fox and Hounds. Ignore the Public Bridleway sign to the left of the inn. The Cleveland Way goes to the left of the white-painted houses beyond, up the right-hand rim of a huge quarry, recently enlarged, which was originally an alum drift. The area you have just passed through was once Guisborough Spa, then alum works, then an iron mine (Spa Wood). The path skirts a wood, then goes along the ridge of Airy Hill, past the farm of that name, and scarcely changes direction till you come out at Saltburn. "Airy" is probably one of our rare Gaelic place-names, brought by those Scandinavians who came from Ireland across the Pennines, and comes from *airighe,* a shieling or hill pasture.

Other famous ironstone mines lie either side of this ridge — Tockets, Upleatham, Chaloner on the west, Margrove (Maggra) Park, Stanghow, Moorsholm, Boosbeck, Lingdale and Kilton on the east. North Skelton was the last to close down, in 1964.

There is a very superior metalled foot-path from Skelton Green to Skelton. At Skelton you go down some steps, then just past a bench turn left down more steps. You pass the Post Office and the County Library, go down past the bus stop, and curve right into the fields again. These are Skelton Castle lands. The Wharton family profited greatly from ironstone royalties. Woods and woodside hedges are beautifully kept. A steep descent through the wood brings you to a mill-pond. The mill-race ran through a wooden aqueduct across the rock-face, and under the great railway viaduct to "Marske Mill", now in ruins. Go up the lane to the left at this point and then turn right into the woods. The upper path will bring you out into the centre of Saltburn, the lower one to the beach and the *Ship Inn.*

Modern Saltburn is a creation of the ironmasters, particularly the Pease family, who persuaded the railway company to extend their line here from Redcar, and to build the imposing *Zetland Hotel,* looking out over the bay to Huntcliff. An 1890 Directory states that "the town is under the government of a local Board, who have carried out all the sanitary arrangements on the most improved principle." Apart from the smaller *Queen Hotel,* there are several private hotels and boarding houses here and in Marske and Redcar. Except perhaps in August accommodation should be easy.

If you have arrived early, and have half a day to spare, it is well worth while spending it along the low coast towards Teesmouth. From Saltburn to South Gare are eight miles of open beach. Take a bus to the Coatham roundabout; then get onto the sands or the

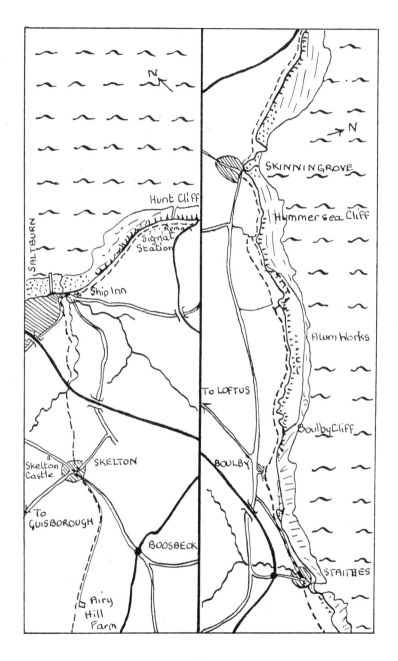

N

Hunt Cliff

Roman
Signal
Station

SALTBURN

Ship Inn

SKELTON

Skelton
Castle

To
GUISBOROUGH

BOOSBECK

Airy
Hill
Farm

SKINNINGROVE

Hummer Sea Cliff

To LOFTUS

Alum Works

BOULBY

Boulby Cliff

STAITHES

N

59

sand-dunes. On your left is industry, old and new, and the busy estuary of the Tees, but to your right is the sea, and the sands are unspoilt. Beneath those sands the remains of an ancient forest were discovered in the 19th century, embedded in peat and blue clay. And it was on Coatham Marshes that the last pocket of resistance against William the Conqueror held out.

The South Gare breakwater jutting out from Tod Point was described after its completion in 1888 as "one of the most gigantic engineering enterprises of modern times". Begun in 1861 it required 4,500,000 tons of slag, apart from cement and other materials. Though in recent years industrial development has taken over vast areas of former waste land, the Tees Estuary is still a fascinating place for bird-watchers.

It is as you walk along the edge of the waves past Redcar and Marske, with Huntcliff and Boulby jutting out as the limit of the sands, that you fully appreciate the great sweep of that bay. On a summer day it looks a safe and harmless coast just here. But even in recent times steamships have been stranded off Coatham promenade, and in the days of sail this bay was the graveyard of hundreds of ships and seamen. In an east or north-east gale the gentle concave from Tod Point to Huntcliff became the most dangerous of lee shores. In three bad gales in 1821, 1824 and 1829 the number of vessels wrecked on the rocks off Redcar was 73.

In the 1830s there was a scheme to build a harbour of refuge to enclose the natural low water harbour formed by the Salt Scar and its parallel ridge of rock on which the pier stands, the Flashes. It was to be called Port William, after William IV, but nothing came of it. Redcar fishermen continued to work from an open coast as they had done in monastic times, "the want of a convenient harbour rendering the pursuit somewhat hazardous."

5.   Saltburn to Whitby — 20 miles.

The cliff path begins in Old Saltburn behind the ancient *Ship Inn*. Below the aristocratic establishments of the high promenade, this corner by Skelton Beck is a strange one. In my youth the beck ran red with ironstone washings, but since the mines closed it is clear again. There is a summer fun-fair, a depressing Victorian mortuary, a few fishing boats on the shingle, and the inn. The curious conical hill "Catnab" may incorporate a Celtic word. The inhabitants "once had an evil reputation for smuggling" and one innkeeper here, Andrews, was an expert at the trade. He was also Master of the

Roxby Hunt. The code-word when a bootleg cargo landed was "Andrew's cow has calved". It is also recorded that someone else hunted hounds "whilst Andrews M.F.H. was in jail".

The path goes up just behind the inn, and keeps to the left of the old Coastguards' Cottages. Soon you are on the cliff edge, high above the sea, and it is as well to look where you are putting your feet. In most places there is nothing to stop you till you hit the rocks or the waves (according to the tide) 400 feet below. These are the cliffs that gave Cleveland its name. Whether you are below them, or above them, never forget for a moment that they are there. At low tide you can walk around the rocky base of the cliffs to Skinningrove, but keep an eye always on the tide and on your watch. There will be rock-pools and caves and fossils that will tempt you to linger. It is a wonderful low-tide world to wander through on a summer's day, but never be tempted to do more than the one headland.

For the walker the cliff-top world is even finer. On a December day the sea may be still as a mill-pond, sea and sky running together in a pearl-grey haze, limpid water lapping the rocks far below. The calls of gull and oyster-catcher are clear against that gentle undertone of a calm sea, and beyond the cliff edge it is a limitless world, with a solitary ship floating dream-like in what you thought was sky. Or the wind may be leaping across from Norway on a clear day, buffeting the sea-birds that love to ride on the cliff-edge currents, and driving white horses before it from a rough looking horizon. In a real north-east gale you might find it difficult to stand at all on the cliff, and the thunder of the great waves smashing against its foot would drown everything else. Spray would come up on the wind and be salt on your lips even at this height.

I will not give any great detail about this cliff-top path which stretches before you now, with small breaks, for some 40 miles. Where there is any doubt, or any alternative, your guess is as good as mine. All you have to do is to keep as near to the sea as possible — and not go over the edge.

On the first promontory of Huntcliff, where the path comes out from the fields onto the cliff itself, just before a concrete pill-box of the last war, is the site of a Roman signal station, one of a series along the Cleveland coast which kept watch against piratical invaders from across the North Sea. Most of this has fallen into the sea now, but part of the rampart ditch can be seen. The fort was excavated in 1912. The antiquarians found fourth century Roman coins and the skeletons of 14 men, women and children, killed when the fort was over-run; the luckless people were thrown head-first

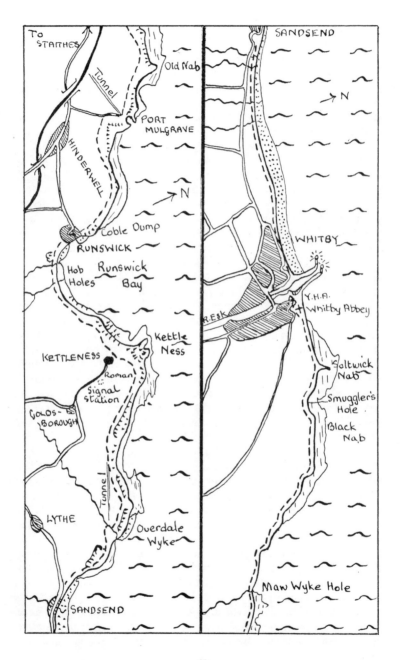

into a well.

Just beyond here the path runs for some way alongside the last stretch of what was formerly one of the most beautiful railway lines in the country. Here begins the long descent down to Skinningrove — a startling place to find on this beautiful coast. But it was at Skinningrove that the main seams of Cleveland ironstone were first found in 1849, though iron had been worked off the cliff faces for many years before that.

Blast furnaces were built here in 1872, and were still working in the early years of the Cleveland Way, creating an extraordinary sight in what must once have been a lovely secluded bay, a miniature Middlesbrough confined between moor and sea, a microcosm of Cleveland in a few acres, and a synopsis of its history. Though some rolling of special steel profiles continues (300 men employed in place of 2,000, and 80% unemployment) the blast furnaces on the cliff top were removed ten years ago and the whole area tidied up.

A well-made path comes down from the beginning of the industrial area to the shore near the old jetty, used until the last war by three ships, one of them called "Cattersty", the name of a wood now lost in slag, and of the sands you come onto. You pass in front of a row of iron miners' or iron workers' cottages — most of the others have now been rebuilt. There is a mining museum at the far end of the village, where the mine was.

Inland beyond the industry, this same valley is lovely still. Kilton Castle was the home of Lucia de Thweng, the "Helen of Cleveland", who left a husband and two lovers to live with Nicholas de Meynell at Whorlton Castle. She married twice more, and after a very eventful life died at Brotton, on the hill above, in 1346, when she was nearing 70 years old.

There is nothing left of old Skinningrove, whose inhabitants "lived more by smuggling than by fishing". The historian Camden noted that some 70 years before he wrote, i.e. in 1607, "they caught a sea-man here who lived upon raw fish for some days, but at last, taking his opportunity, he made his escape into his own element." A more dangerous visitor in 1779 was the American Paul Jones, who fired a few cannon balls into the bay. In Camden's time "Skengrave" throve "by the great variety of fish which it takes". For many years there have been no full-time fishermen here, but part-time cobles still go out from the beach.

Though you may glance back at Skinningrove with incredulity, you will be glad to climb the steep cliff out of it, onto the headland of Hummersea. Both here and on Huntcliff in the bend of the railway occurs the place-name Warsett, which may be a rare Cleveland use of the Norse word *Saeter,* a summer pasture, such as occurs more frequently in the Dales — Burtersett and Appersett.

In the next bay, a steep path leads down to a tiny low-tide beach. Two ponds on the cliff edge have what seems to be the very old name of Snilah. They are reputed to be bottomless. From them you can either go a field inland by Warren Cottages to the path over the summit of Boulby, or you can find a way through the Warren itself, almost on the face of the cliff.

This face walk is fantstic. Boulby, the highest cliff in England, has been quarried out for building stone, for ironstone, for alum and for jet and now between the upper cliff and the sea-cliff edge you walk in a strange world of forgotten and half-obliterated industry. Here are two circles of dressed stone — alum soaking pits. There are great blocks of undressed stone preserving across the centuries the sand-rippled of an ancient beach. The Lias shales can be seen, with lumps of crude coal. The foundations of some old building cling crazily to the cliff edge. Eventually the steep and shaly face of Lingberry Hill above Rockliff (local pronunciation Rawcliff — "Red Cliff") will bar your way, and it is safer to pick a way carefully onto the top path, at the edge of cultivation. There is one place where quarrymen have cut steps in an easy rock, but there are some grass slopes further back that anyone could walk up. The alum north of Lingberry went down to an alum house at Hummersea, and was shipped from the bay there.

At the other side again, above Boulby itself, are more acres of old alum works. In the hamlet of Boulby there is a fine old barn on the left which has the foundations of many of the old alum-working buildings round it. The barn was used for pit-ponies from the Boulby iron mine and there is in it one of the biggest beams I have ever seen — over 30 ft. long and some 18 inches square. The alum shale was calcined, then soaked in the stone-lined pits. The liquid was piped into stone culverts and wooden troughs, perhaps with pumps in places, and so into the alum house where it was boiled in copper cauldrons, an alkali was added and the mixture was re-boiled to get the alum precipitated. Alum was shipped to London — and urine brought back from there for use as alkali, though it was said not to be so strong as the local variety!

The alum shales are naturally bituminous, and sometimes catch fire spontaneously. As a boy I sometimes saw these strange fires burning high up on that cliff above the sea. Waste from both Boulby and Grinkle mines came out of or over the cliff here too. The whole hill is honey-combed with passages. One old iron-miner from Staithes told me how from the Skinningrove mine he could come through onto the cliff at Boulby and go home by cliff or shore. Once after firing a shot he broke through into a smugglers' cave. There were just a couple of planks in it, and an empty cask. Armstrongs farm at Boulby Grange, and they will tell you of an underground passage, long blocked up, from a "Gin Hole" below to the Grange cellars. A green track goes on from Boulby, a field away from the cliff edge now, and soon you are going down Cowber Lane into Staithes itself.

You cannot pass quickly through Staithes. You certainly will not want to. There is the *Cod and Lobster,* fronting the tiny harbour, outfacing the sea itself — and many a time the sea has been in its cellars. You might be forviven for thinking that Staithes men would not notice a bit of salt in their beer, for they seem part and parcel of the sea. Shut off from the interior by its steep bank and narrow valley, clinging house above house to the cliff face, Staithes was for centuries a closed community where the coastal dialect of Cleveland lingered on in its purest forms, incomprehensible to a stranger. Half the families were Verrills or Theeakers. Until 30 years ago the women commonly wore their traditional bonnets.

When James Cook was an apprentice grocer here, 50 fishing cobles sailed from Staithes. Even now, alone of the small villages of this coast, Staithes retains its character as a working community of fishermen. There are still five large cobles going out full-time fishing, and many more part-time boats.

A traditional Staithes dish is ling-pie, and here "ling" is a fish, not heather.

A dish for onny king
Is yan o them ling pies;
Steeas wimmin — an they're wise —
Knaws what ti deea wi ling;
Neea lass sud git her ring
Till a ling pie she tries;
A dish for onny king,
Is yan o them ling pies!

On September 11th, 1866, was held the "Great Coble Race" from Staithes to Whitby, between a famous Northumberland crew, the Blyth miners in *Temperance Star,* and a crew of Staithes fishermen in *Jane,* for a Silver Cup, £100 a side, "and the Championship of the North Sea." Crowds thronged the cliffs to see this race over 10 miles of open sea, the result of a challenge and bets in a Whitby inn. The Staithes crew — Thomas Coll, Simon Robinson, Thomas Crooks and Burton Verrill — won in 1 hour 25½ minutes and said they would have rowed to Flamborough Head! They lifted up their heavy oars and danced on the coble thofts (seats) in Whitby Harbour.

Inland from Staithes goes another smugglers' track, on a narrow ridge between two deep valleys — Rigg Lane. At Scaling this links with old tracks over the moors to Fryup and Danby. A wonderful alternative to the semi-industrial areas between Guisborough and Boulby is to follow the moors from Highcliff to Danby and then go in to Staithes by Rigg Lane. Potash mining is the latest threat to this area, but beyond Staithes — and the longer you stay in Staithes the more reluctant you will be ever to leave it — you are away from the main ironstone area. The cliff path goes off from the top of Church Street (don't look for a church — there isn't one!) which rises steeply from the *Cod and Lobster*. You can get round the cliff edge by Penny Nab, Jet Wyke and old Nab, but the proper path goes over fields to Brackenberry Wyke and then past the site of the old Hinderwell Beacon.

Below here is Port Mulgrave where ironstone from the Grinkle mine was once loaded. The next headland is called Lingrow, and Lingra Knock is a reef in the sea below. Another unusual place name a little further on is Coble Dump. *Dump* is Old Norse for a pit or pool. Here the paths turns sharp right away from the cliff to the top of Runswick Bank. Paths direct down from headland to bay are difficult and dangerous.

Runswick is a delightfully situated village, on the headland's southern slopes — a sun-trap when the sun shines. According to the Cleveland historian Ord "160 years ago i.e. 1684, the whole village except one house sank in the night. Great loss of life must have ensued had not some fishermen been engaged at the time in waking a corpse. The alarm was quickly given and the inhabitants escaped with the loss of their houses and property." Thirty years ago there were still working boats and nets on the steep wooden slipway here, but now Runswick is entirely a holiday and week-end village.

Beyond Hob Holes (where the Hob of Hob Hole was said to cure whooping cough) the path goes on to the prominent headland of Kettleness by Catbeck Hill and Catbeck Trod. This is a headland you can spend hours exploring, among old alum and ironstone works. Rock scars jut out into the sea. Before you go into Loop Wyke beyond, between "Scratch Alley" and Goldsborough village is another of the Roman coastal forts. Excavated in 1919 this was found to have had 4 ft. walls. In a well in the SE corner were found three human skulls and the bones of oxen and spaniels or sheepdogs. In the inner room the skeleton of a short, thick-set man lay stretched on the open hearth. Near its feet the skeleton of a taller man was found lying face down, and beneath it the skeleton of a large and powerful dog, its head thrust against the man's throat and its paws across his shoulders. In that last desperate fight the dog had killed one of his master's slayers before being himself killed. The floor was covered with the remains of bread, oxen, goats, pigs, deer, hares, rabbits, crabs, mussels, limpets, whelks and winkles. Coins were of the period 392-423.

Tellgreen Hill leads on to Overdale Wyke and Deepgrove Wyke, where something of a detour is needed to get onto the old railway line that comes out of a long tunnel here. There is a footpath through the field and onto Lythe Bank, but the better route now is to follow the line round Sandsend Ness and into Sandsend itself. On the Ness were some of the oldest alum workings, going back to the first years of the 17th century.

Sandsend Wyke is also known as Dunsley Bay after the small village slightly inland where the Roman Road over Wheeldale Moor is thought to have ended — the bay being the Dunum Sinus of Roman times. It is here that the Esk came out before the Ice Age.

If the tide is out there is a fine walk along the beach but otherwise you might just as well take a bus. Your time can be better spent in Whitby itself than in walking on along the old line and the promenade.

Whitby would need a book to itself, and several have already been written. The old boatyards where Cook's ships were built, the herring fleet, the museum — you had better allow another week here.

I wish I were in Whitby town
* Now lilacs bloom in Flowergate —*
I wish I were in Whitby town,
Where crooked streets go up and down
* From Church Street or from Baxtergate —*
The coble sails are warm and brown
And golden sunshine glances down
* On red roofs smiling everywhere —*

There is a youth hostel near the Abbey. Ample other accommodation is available *(Seacliffe Hotel,* Whitby; *Seaside Hotel).*

6.   Whitby to Scarborough — 18 miles.

After the 199 steps that lead to church and abbey you are glad to pause by Caedmon's monument. It is pleasing to remember that in 1394-5 one eighth of the Abbey's expenditure was incurred for malt and wine and of all the Abbey's servants the brewer drew the highest wages! Among other purchases were 1,000 herrings, two barrels of eels, three pike and a porpoise. There were also dates, currants, figs, mace and pepper — and one item "for working fourteen wolves' skins—1s. 9d".

By Saltwick Nab and Bay and another Smugglers' Hole near Black Nab the path keeps more or less to the edge of high steep cliffs. At Whitestones Point is a lighthouse and the "Whitby Bull", whose four blasts every 90 seconds during foggy weather can be heard a very long way.

Beyond Hawsker Bottoms, the magnificent view of Robin Hood's Bay opens out. It is three miles across from North Cheek to South Cheek, the 600 ft. cliff of Ravenscar. "Bay" has long been the haunt of artists. It is beautiful, but it is dead. The affluent society has moved in, and the fishermen have long since moved out, although in 1974 one coble was again fishing. I remember nets spread out across Wayfoot above the tiny "dock" just before the war — for the last time. The *Bay Hotel* once had a ship wrecked against it! Robin Hood may have visited these parts, but "Robin Hood's Butts" on the moor above are Bronze Age round barrows probably named after some hob, Robin Goodfellow.

When the tide is out by far the best thing is to walk along the beach and scar round the bay; when waves are breaking in the main street, follow a path up an alley opposite the *Bay Hotel* to the youth hostel at Boggle Hole. There is a rich variety of fossils to be found all along the foot of the cliffs to Ravenscar itself where steps lead up to the hotel (site of another Roman station) and the village, where the Lyke Wake Walks ends. Ravenscar is probably the only coastal village to have rights of peat-cutting on the moor behind. The rights are still exercised. There was a very big alum works here which worked well into the 19th century.

The cliffs at Ravenscar and beyond are a geologist's paradise. Even if you are not a geologist they are some of the finest, though not the highest, on the walk. The views towards Scarborough are magnificent, with headland jutting out after headland. Beyond the deep cove of Blea Wyke is Beast Cliff, where an English king is said to have been shipwrecked about the 12th century. At Hayburn Wyke a waterfall comes down onto the shore, and a new wooden bridge crosses the gully. Through the wood is an hotel and in front of it near the old station stones mark a prehistoric encampment. Hayburn Wyke is a much-frequented spot, but you may come into it on a day when it seems still a corner of ancient unspoilt beauty.

About a mile past here a lane goes into Cloughton Newlands and

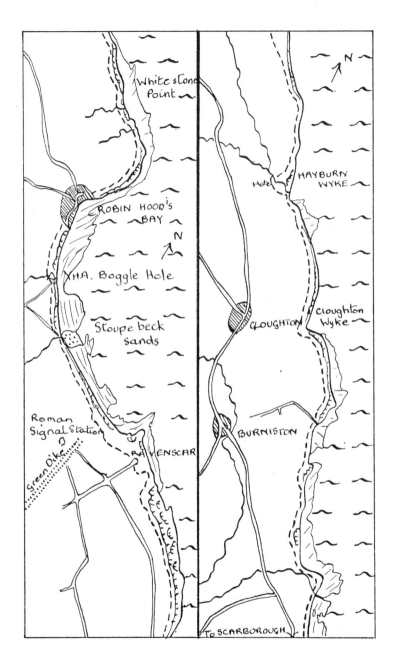

Whitestone Point

HAYBURN WYKE

Hotel

ROBIN HOOD'S BAY

N

YHA. Boggle Hole

CLOUGHTON

Cloughton Wyke

Stoupe beck sands

Roman Signal Station

Green Dike

RAVENSCAR

BURNISTON

TO SCARBOROUGH

in another three miles, past Cloughton Wyke, and Hundale Point, you are at Scalby and the beginning of Scarborough.

The Scandinavian *Kormakssaga* relates how "the brothers Thorgils and Kormak went harrying in Ireland, Wales, England and Scotland and were accounted the most excellent of men. They were the first to set up the stronghold called Scarborough", after Thorgil's nickname of Skarthi, "the hare-lip". This was in 966 but Bronze and Iron Age remains have been found on the present castle site.

Scarborough is a fine town, with a fine harbour and a fine history. But it is a town — much more a town than Whitby is — and at this stage of the walk you will not want to linger here. There is a youth hostel and ample other accommodation.

7.   Scarborough to Filey — 8 miles.

The last stage of the "Cleveland Way", with the old boundary of Cleveland left far behind at Whitby, begins at the end of the South Bay promenade, above the sea bathing pool. The cliffs are lower now but curve pleasantly round in three bays to Filey Brigg. The bays are Cornelian (after the stones sometimes found there), Cayton and Gristhorpe. The northern tip of Cornelian Bay is White Nab, below which are the Perilous Rocks. Cayton Bay begins at Osgodby Point and in it are the Calf Allen Rocks. All these villages are ancient — Osgodby was Asgozbi in Domesday Book (ON name *Asgautr*), Cayton was Caitun (an English name here — Caega's farm), Gristhorpe was Grisetorp — Gris's village (ON personal name from *griss,* a pig).

Unless the sky and the sea are very blue this gentle stroll will be something of an anti-climax after all that has gone before. At high tide you may even have to take to the main road for a short way but usually you can drop down through the woods near Osgodby Point to the sands of Cayton Bay and climb up again to Killerby and Lebberston Cliffs. Civilisation crowds in with camps and caravan sites but there is one cove where sea buckthorn gives a vivid display of orange berries in autumn, and there is general improvement as you near Filey. Below Yons Nab are the Horseshoe Rocks — and a mile further on the Old Horse Rocks. Then from Filey's North Cliff you can look out over Brigg and Bay to Bempton Cliffs and Flamborough Head, one of the finest views of all with which to end your walk.

The narrow headland that goes out to the Brigg is called Carr

A Cleveland hob

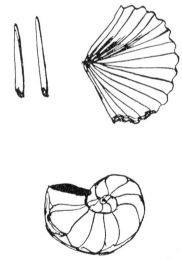

Fosslis found in Cleveland

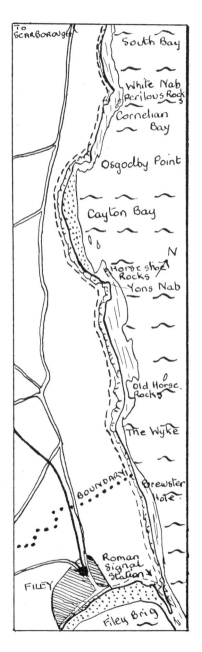

Naze, Carr probably coming from the Ancient British word *caer,* a camp. In August 1857 a deluge of rain caused tremendous damage all along this coast, and part of the cliff here collapsed revealing the foundations of a Roman fort — another of the chain of signal stations. Filey's spa, a chalybeate spring, is also here.

There are ways down the rock cliffs to the Brigg — but be careful. The best parts of Filey are the Brigg, and the quay where the cobles are drawn up. This is a pleasant town in which to end the walk — rather like a seaside Helmsley. But you need not end it here. If you have time and inclination you can walk on along the magnificent cliffs of Speeton and Bempton, where the cliff-climbers used to gather sea-birds' eggs, to Flamborough Head and Bridlington. And then you can follow the Wold Gate — T'Waud Yat — to Kilham, and find a way over Duggleby Wold back to Malton and Helmsley, or go on to Wetwang and get a bus to York. But whatever you do now, you have covered a good hundred miles of the finest country I know. I hope you enjoyed it as much as I have done.